Research Papers

Research Papers:
A Beginner's Manual

Pearl G. Aldrich

Frostburg State College, Maryland

Winthrop Publishers, Inc.

Cambridge, Massachusetts

Library of Congress Cataloging in Publication Data

Aldrich, Pearl G
   Research papers.

  1. Report writing.   2. Research.   3. Study, Method of.   I. Title.
LB2369.A56   808'.023   76–954
ISBN 0–87626–754–1

Acknowledgments

"The Hectic Life of the Alpha Bull," pp. 57–59. Reprinted from PSYCHOL-OGY TODAY Magazine, October 1974. Copyright © 1974. Ziff-Davis Publishing Company. All rights reserved.

"Television News as News," pp. 65–67. From TELEVISION NEWS, copyright © 1968 by Irving E. Fang, by permission of Hastings House, Publishers.

For my students,
  Whose questions generated these answers.

Contents

Foreword

It is an old New England custom to label plainly all the small, inconspicuous side streets in town. But strangers can drive the length of the main thoroughfare without seeing a sign to identify it. When they finally defy traffic to stop and ask, the native will answer, "Why, Massachusetts Avenue," clearly implying, "Everybody *knows* that."

The textbooks I used—and then stopped using—to teach the craft of the research paper all included necessary and usable information. However, they omitted, like New Englanders, the name of the main street. These omissions implied that everybody *knows* the answers to the types of questions that my students ask most frequently: "How can I summarize and quote without plagiarizing?" or "Why is *PMLA* a more valuable source than the book review in the local paper?" The omissions also implied that everybody *knows* how to document media sources such as television newscasts, commercial records, and tapes; for what purposes to use quoted material; and even simple, but invaluable information such as how to type the footnotes so they look like the models in the book.

This manual is unusual because it is not predicated on the New Englander's "everybody knows" assumption. Its content is selected and presented with the recognition that college students writing research papers are usually strangers on unknown streets, and it offers a clearly marked road map. Like a good guide, it provides necessary information crisply and without condescension.

This is a text I won't stop using. Whether you are teacher or student, neither will you.

Lucille G. Shandloff

Coordinator, Basic English Program
Hunter College, New York City

Research Papers

Why the Research Paper Assignment?

Investigating a subject, thinking through the point you want to make, organizing the evidence to support it, and writing it in the research paper form is the most versatile single assignment any course of study can offer you. Years later, people remember with pleasure not only the information they gathered, but also how good it felt to dig into an interesting subject on their own. In addition, the research paper assignment pays long-term dividends in developing your thought processes and ability to handle abstract ideas, as well as methods of organizing time and materials.

The research paper is basically an experience in finding evidence and using it to make something of your own. Although you use other people's ideas and some of their writing, your paper is not just a mechanical compilation of their thoughts. By synthesizing, blending, and arranging portions of materials already available, you produce an individual product and make an individual statement. For example, if you make a bookcase, you do not grow the tree in order to cut the shelves. You make a plan and use materials already available. You choose among types of wood, decide upon appropriate lengths according to your plan, pick the proper kinds of nails, find the right glue for that wood, and decide upon the color of paint. In the end, it is your own product. So it is with the research paper. You make the plan, seek out the materials, pick and choose among them, organize appropriate portions, and from them make your own statement.

1

As you work through the steps that produce a research paper, your thought processes are constantly in action, performing the immediate tasks and developing scope for future use. For example, you will do a great deal of mental sorting of abstract ideas. You will sort usable ideas from the unusable, the important from the unimportant. You will sort out like ideas and group them. You will sort opinion from fact in your sources and then in your writing. You will sort the strong, vivid words in your writing from the dull, drab, and inappropriate. The result will be improved ability to think through problems in an orderly, progressive way.

Because investigation requires a variety of steps, the research paper assignment also improves your methods of organizing time and materials. Your time for doing the work must be divided into portions of your day and week so that all your activities will have their balanced proportion of attention. Following a written working schedule will be helpful here. Bibliography cards, notes, spontaneously written paragraphs of your own reflections must be organized to prevent confusion and loss of time when the material is needed to act as fuel for your mental processes. At the same time, the ideas emerging from the mental processes must be carefully arranged so that, at the end, the physical organization and intellectual organization will be so blended that the paper will be a homogenized whole.

Another reason the research paper assignment is made regularly is that it teaches you to work freely within a given structure. The mechanical details of footnotes, bibliography, and physical form of the paper are all set by tradition and custom. In addition, reasonably formal written language is expected. Within this structure, you are urged to move freely among the ideas, accepting and discarding those of others, and generating your own. Working within the inherited structure—including the data required and excluding that not required—sharpens your powers of observation and control of detail. These techniques are valuable not only for the individual assignment and for other classes, but also for life in general. For example, you are born into an inherited social structure. As you grow up, you accept and discard parts of your parents' way of life, generating your own. When you accept a job, you step into an inherited commercial structure, but your individuality is expressed in how you do the job until it becomes something of your own.

A final and important benefit that the research paper assignment provides is practice in self-discipline, in planning and pacing your work so that your paper is mature and thoughtful. The hasty writing about undigested ideas that results from a last-minute scramble of cut classes and sleepless nights is easily identifiable. It is disappointing to receive and dreary to read. The student who worked that way misses the fine glow that comes from turning in his or her best effort and usually feels worse about the final product than the instructor.

The following step-by-step guidance will help you investigate, organize, and write your paper in the most efficient and timesaving way that this project can be done. If you follow the steps as outlined, your paper should be well accepted by your professor and will pay you all the dividends available from such a versatile assignment.

Step–by–Step
Procedure

Part I

PRELIMINARY THOUGHT

Step 1: The Subject

Usually, the research paper assignment is made fairly early in the course, with a due date close to the end. Before you are expected to begin work, however, you will be introduced to a range of possibilities for acceptable subjects. Your instructor may provide a list from which to choose or you may have free choice from among subjects that interest you.

Once you have chosen a general area for your paper, the first step is to limit the subject to a size that you can handle based on the point you want to make, length of paper, time in which to do it, and material available in your library. However, many beginners choose subjects that are so wide, so general, so all-inclusive—for example: drugs, politics, movies, art—that if they wrote twenty volumes each, they would not be able to complete their work in a lifetime. The following procedure, therefore, will help narrow your subject appropriately:

1. With your general subject in mind, answer this question:

What point do you want to make?

In this manual, we are using the phrase "point you want to make" because it is clear, exact, and not technical. However, there are other phrases for the same thing. Some variants of the question above include the following: What is the controlling idea? What is the purpose of the paper? What conclusion do you intend to reach? What are you going to prove? What is your thesis statement? They all mean much the same.

It is possible to make only one major point per paper. It is the main idea that you wish to leave in the reader's mind. Your library research will provide evidence to illustrate and support that major point. When writing the paper, you will probably make several minor points because they contribute to the major one; however, throughout the project, concentrate on the major point. If you keep it firmly in mind and before the reader, the other points will fall into their appropriate places. Answer the question above as specifically as possible, then follow the procedure that follows, and you will have a workable subject.

Sometimes a student who is very interested in current topics will find that his or her particular approach does not yet exist. If this happens to you, store your idea until you are working for a Ph.D., and make your individual statement then. Or, if events about your subject are too recent for books or thoughtful analyses to be published yet, ask your instructor if you may use newspapers, news magazines, and television documentaries as your sources. If you may, the documentaries will be most difficult to see, particularly so that you can take notes. There are suppliers who rent documentaries that appeared in the past, if you have the funds and the film can reach you in time. If one is to be broadcast in the near future, tape record the audio through a plug-in jack or, lacking that, use a hand microphone and keep everybody quiet. The tape, with publication data from the credits, will provide what you need for the paper.

Let us follow the procedure to narrow a wide subject, with history as the example. Q: What point do you want to make? A: I want to discuss the Revolutionary War.

Your subject is now limited to a specific era and a specific event, but it is still too large to cover in a one-course paper. Therefore, ask yourself the following questions to further narrow the subject. The key words are italicized.

2. *What* aspects of the Revolutionary War do you wish to discuss? Well, it had causes. It had results. It had problems. It had major issues. It had personalities of interest in both military and diplomatic posts. It also had many, many other aspects that you could list. We'll use "problems" to continue our example.

3. What *kinds* of problems? A few answers that come to mind quickly include the following: The problems of spies during the Revolutionary War. The problems of financing the Revolutionary War. The problems of recruitment during the Revolutionary War. The problems of the people who remained loyal to the British king. The problems of involvement of foreign powers during the Revolutionary War.

For many assignments, any one of the above could be sufficiently limited. However, the shorter the paper, the more highly specialized the subject must be; therefore, you might have to scale it down a little more. You can further reduce the size of the subject by placing it in time or space or by identifying people, according to the following additional questions:

4. *When* were the problems most troublesome?

When was the financing handled or the money raised?

When were the spies most active?

5. *Where* were the problems most troublesome?

Where was the financing handled or talked about?

Where was the money for the troops raised?

Where were the spies concentrated or most active?

6. *How* were the problems most troublesome?

How was the financing handled?

How was the money for the troops raised?

How were the spies most active?

7. *Who* handled or identified or caused the most troublesome problems?

Who was involved with the financing, in one way or another?

Who raised or provided the money for the troops?

Who were the spies?

8. The final step for limiting your subject is to return to the original question. What point do you want to make about the Revolutionary War? The answer will give you a specific and limited subject for your paper.

Step 2: Gathering Preliminary General Information

This step consists mostly of fast reading, with only general notetaking. It will give you a quick overview of your subject and enough general information to do Steps 3 and 4. When you finish this step, you should see your subject in broad terms and you will be able, if necessary, to mold it to fit what is available in your library.

If this paper is for a course about a specific subject, such as American History from the Colonial Period to the Civil War, Introduction to Psychology, Anthropological Studies of the American Indian of the Southwest, or something similarly limited, the first part of this step is to read your textbook, specifically the chapter or section that covers your topic. Usually you will find a list of books and articles at the end of the chapter or at the back of the book.

If this is the general English course in which you write a research paper primarily to learn the techniques and library resources, start with the encyclopedias for your quick overview. Encyclopedias should never be used as "research" sources later in your education than the tenth grade, but they are useful now to give you this quick, general overview. In addition, they also provide lists of magazine articles and books at the ends of their articles.

Encyclopedias and reference works are divided into two major categories: general and specialized.

- *General*

Encyclopedia Britannica: Articles written by scholars who use technical vocabularies and complex sentence structures.

Encyclopedia Americana: Articles written for high school graduates with slightly better than average reading vocabularies.

World Book: Written primarily for elementary school students. Material presented as simply as possible, but not very deeply or thoroughly. Lots of pictures.

Collier's Encyclopedia: Written for the average citizen who has been out of school for several years. Articles are very general.

Columbia Encyclopedia and *Lincoln Encyclopedia:* One volume each. Material very limited and frequently out of date.

- *Specialized*

Specialized encyclopedias, dictionaries, handbooks, yearbooks, and other informative volumes exist for almost every subject, trade, profession, hobby, person, or object of interest to humanity. In the past thirty years, specialized encyclopedias ranging from one to thirty-six volumes have been published covering all the liberal arts subjects, all the sciences, mathematics, and engineering. They can be invaluable in this step. The following random list is presented to show both the range and how special specialization can get. It is a very small fraction of the total available, arranged in no special order.

Who's Who in America
Current Biography
Twentieth Century Authors
Short Story Index
Cyclopedia of American Government
Encyclopedia of Painting
The Electrician's Handbook
Civil Engineer's Manual
Bee Keeper's Encyclopedia
American Nicknames
The World of Business
Forestry Handbook
Food, The Yearbook of Agriculture
Larousse's Encyclopedia of World Geography
Dictionary of Film Makers
An Actor's Guide to the Talkies
A Directory of Children's Theatres in the United States
Who Done It: A Guide to Detective Mystery Fiction
Encyclopedia of American History
Encyclopedia of Jazz
Encyclopedia of Religion
Encyclopedia of Advertising
Grove's Dictionary of Music and Musicians
Encyclopedia of Banking and Finance
Encyclopedia of World Politics
The Fun Encyclopedia
Who's Who in Oz

Harper's Encyclopedia of Science
The Women's Rights Movement in the United States 1848–
    1970
The Encyclopedia of Morals
Crowell's Handbook of Contemporary Drama
Woman Media: Current Resources About Women
Who Wrote the Movie and What Else Did He Write?

After you have skimmed enough general and specialized sources to give you the size and shape of your topic,
turn it over in your mind. Think deliberately about the way
you want to approach the paper, then do other things and let
your subconscious go to work for you. The subconscious, or
wherever thought processes take place, is a great help in
mental digestion. A few days later, when you think deliberately about the topic again, you will find some decisions
already made and much material organized in your mind.

Step 3: Deciding the Kind of Research Paper to Write

There are several major kinds of research papers, some of
which may be applicable to the current assignment; some,
to another. All of them are usable, although a few are more
popular than others. Read through the definitions and
decide which kind would best fit your subject.

Kinds of Research Papers

1. Prove or disprove a theory, idea, or conclusion
    This is the most popular. In it, you establish the
theory, idea, or conclusion, then present information pro

and con. At the end, you make a decision either for or against the subject and give your own opinion. If you decide that there is some good and some bad in the subject, you report that decision and tell why you've reached it as part of the conclusion.

2. Descriptive

As the name indicates, you describe all aspects of a subject, usually a contemporary problem, process, or situation. After you identify the subject fully, you describe what is being done, techniques being used, results being obtained, and, depending upon the specific subject, prospects for the future. Personal opinion expressed in a descriptive paper can be approval, disapproval, and/or suggestions for improvement. Or, you need not express an opinion.

3. Compare and contrast

In this kind of paper, you summarize and group the contrasts and comparisons among authoritative opinions about the subject. If you wish, you can express your agreement or disagreement with the opinions, or make it a report in which you make no decision.

4. Cause and effect

In this type of paper, you establish the cause, then report the major effects. It can be a status quo report, or at the end, you may give your own opinion about the extent of good and bad effects and decide whether the cause should stay or go as part of our culture.

5. Explanatory or a this-is-what-happened report of a major event or series of events

This is a particularly interesting kind of paper if there are conflicting reports about what happened. You can document the conflicts and reach a conclusion about which one or which combination seems to be the most probable, or you can leave it as a report, indicating that the conflict has never been resolved. If there is no conflict, the major work is searching out various reports of the events and piecing the sequence together.

6. Biographical

As the name states, a biographical paper tells the story of a person's life, usually an important and influential person. This is primarily a report paper, with no opportunity for personal opinion unless you decide that the person's reputation is not justified or that recognition of his/her achievements has been neglected.

7. Historical or chronological development of an invention, idea, theory, country, industry, religion, school of thought, or anything that has a history

This is a report paper that documents how something, either physical or intellectual, developed into the form that we now know.

8. Technical

These papers are usually done in science and engineering courses. You perform an experiment, then report the results. The beginning of the paper can give a survey of reports of previous experiments that were similar, or it can start with the experimental procedures.

9. Literary (print or film)

a. Reaction paper. In this one, you report critical reactions published in magazine and newspaper reviews about a novel, play, or film.

b. Evaluation paper. After you have read a piece of fiction, present evaluations of the work from writings of literary scholars. This can be a report paper or it may include your agreement or disagreement with the opinions you report.

c. Analysis paper. In this paper, you analyze the work you have read or seen according to standard criteria such as characterization, symbolism, or structure.

After you have decided upon the kind of paper you wish to write, you are ready for the next step.

Step 4: Statement of Controlling Purpose

This step will clarify the point you want to make in your paper. It will also show how well you sorted out your ideas during the preliminary reading, and it is the time when the results of your mental digestion become useful.

In one paragraph, state the point you want to make in the paper, with brief listing of the evidence you will use to support it. This statement, with only minor changes, should remain the controlling idea throughout.

The following are several examples:

```
     I want to show what influenced the music of
Frank Zappa. I will discuss the type of music that
was important when he was young and how the styles of
composers of classical music, like Varèse, Webern, and
Stravinsky, influenced him.
```

```
     The point I want to make is how Woman's Lib got
started.  To do that, I will read about Mary Wollstonecraft
and Margaret Fuller from the 19th century and Betty Friedan
and Gloria Steinem in the 20th century.
```

```
     The point I want to make is that Whitman's life-
style was not put into his poetry, particularly all that
about the divinity of bodily functions, like sex.  It was
probably all wishful thinking.  I'll contrast sections
of Song of Myself with the way he really lived.
```

```
     Who really built the stone statues on Easter Island
is what I want to write about.  I don't know yet which
theory I'll agree with, but I'll investigate the ones
given by Thor Heyerdahl and A. Metraux.
```

As you can see from the examples, the students did enough preliminary reading to discover specific information to support their main point. Your statement should be similar and, with only minor changes, should remain the controlling idea throughout both your research and writing.

Now that you have decided on a subject, narrowed and limited it as necessary, obtained an overview, chosen the kind of paper you want to write, and clarified the point you want to make by writing a short paragraph, you are ready to tackle the sources.

Part II

THE SOURCES

Step 5: Preparing the Working Bibliography

The word *bibliography* is used in two ways in connection with a research paper. One is for this step—a working bibliography which changes content as you investigate. The other is for one of the last steps—the bibliography page which is the final list of sources that you actually used and which you will place on a separate page at the end of the completed paper. The latter will be described in its proper order. During this step, we will deal with the working bibliography, a collection of *possible* sources of information about your subject.

The working bibliography changes content frequently. First you list possibilities; then you check to see if they are appropriate to your topic. In this process, some sources are discarded, new ones are added, and the final group is your usable bibliography. To start, then, you collect possibilities in the following customary manner.

It is traditional to use 3 × 5 index cards for bibliography work and to write the publishing information about each source on separate cards according to a specific order. When recorded in the proper order, the information can later be used, accurately and easily, in footnote forms and on the final bibliography page.

To avoid backtracking constantly use the following procedure:

1. Collect at least three times the minimum number of required sources for your paper. When you investigate these possibilities, some won't have the information you need, others will be duplications, still others will not be available to you. Therefore, you will efficiently save yourself a last minute scramble if you start with three times the number you will need.

2. Collect your possible sources from several types of publications. The varieties and their characteristics are described in the next section, *Types of Sources*. Occasionally, a specific type of source will be eliminated by your instructor. Some will prefer serious magazines to popular magazines, for example. Others might prefer that you use all print sources and no films or records.

It's also possible that sources for a particular subject might be limited to one type of publication; newspaper articles, for example. Before you invest much time in such a subject, discuss the problem with your instructor. Unless you have specific permission to do so, do not use only one kind of publication. It's like painting yourself into a corner. Use a variety.

All the work for Step 5 usually is done in the reference room or reference section of the library, unless specialized catalogues, such as the film catalogues or government documents, are located elsewhere.

Collecting a working bibliography usually draws upon your supply of faith and hope, with some charitable thoughts needed for the limitations of catalogue makers. In the various catalogues from which you will collect your possible sources, you will find only titles under the subject headings covering your topic. You will not find a description of the contents of a magazine article and only rarely a useful description of the contents of a book; therefore, you will have to hope that the item will be useful. This is the main reason a working bibliography changes content. However, it would be unnecessarily time consuming to run down each publication when you find the title to determine its usefulness. You search out each one individually only after you have collected a large group of *possible* sources.

Types of Sources

Sources for research papers are divided into two general types—primary sources and secondary sources.

Primary sources are the novels, short stories, plays, or poetry written by an author, if you are preparing a literary paper. For example, a paper about James Dickey would include quotations from his poems or, possibly, his novel, *Deliverance,* and the film made from the book. These are the primary sources. The secondary sources are the articles and books other people have written about Dickey's work. Your paper itself would be considered a secondary source because you are writing about Dickey and his work.

If you are writing a paper about the incidence of alcoholism among students and prepare a questionnaire to be answered by a hundred local students, the data you derive from the answers would be a primary source. If your topic is in chemistry and you perform experiments to find answers to a specific problem, the results of the experiment would be a primary source. If you choose a topic in eighteenth-century music and quote a passage from a Mozart score, the score would be a primary source. In addition, an interview, a lecture, or personal correspondence with an inventor, the writer, an experimenter, an originator of a theory, or a major scientist are considered primary sources.

By a large majority, however, research papers such as yours are based upon secondary sources. Secondary sources are print and electronic publications *about* a subject by someone other than the originator of the ideas, experiments, theories, or literature.

All published books and periodicals, all released films and recordings available to the public are not equal in value. They are particularly unequal when you are working on research papers because you need authoritative statements about your topic. Would-be authorities are published in many disguises and frequently appear to the casual eye to be more authoritative than the people who know most about the subject. Publications by would-be authorities are generally easier to find in most libraries than the works of the real authorities. The works of real authorities are usually found in college, university, and very large metropolitan public libraries that can afford massive holdings. Granted that expert judgment about reliability of sources comes after many years of study, it is, nevertheless, possible to make reasonable judgments about the values of various types of publications by applying the guidelines set up in the following discussion.

Secondary sources can be divided into the following four main categories:

1. Scholarly and professional
2. Serious
3. Popular
4. Exploitive

Of these categories, scholarly, professional, and serious publications are always acceptable sources for research papers. Some popular publications are acceptable; others, not. These distinctions will be discussed and illustrated in the section defining the popular category. The exploitive publications should never be used as sources. The following descriptions of the four categories and where they overlap will serve as a guide for your judgment.

1. Scholarly and professional

Scholarly and professional publications are written by experts who have spent years studying their subjects. Their approach to their subject is wide, factual, and unemotional. They support their ideas with sufficient information to convince others as knowledgeable as themselves, and they always provide their sources. The majority of the books are published by university presses; some, by publishing companies that handle highly specialized subjects; a few, by prestigious commercial publishers. The journals or magazines are published by professional associations and subscriptions to them are covered by membership dues. Most college libraries and large public libraries subscribe to the professional journals in most fields.

Advising you in general about using scholarly publications is tricky because of the following contradiction: Most scholars and experts write for readers with extensive background in the same field, frequently use highly specialized vocabularies, and make references with no explanation to ideas and other publications that everybody in the field knows. On the other hand, many of these publications can be valuable to beginners for whom the material will be informative and form a foundation for further study. Use depends upon both the book or article and your interest in the subject.

One way around this problem, if a specific publication proves too specialized for you, is to see if there is a version written for the general public. For example, during the past decade there has been great interest in the study of dreams. W. C. Dement and N. Kleitman's article "The Relation of Eye Movements During Sleep to Dream Activity: An Objective Method for the Study of Dreaming," which appeared in the *Journal of Experimental Psychology*, is a highly specialized report. However, books such as *Experimental Studies of Dreaming*, edited by H. A. Witkin and H. B. Lewis, fall into the serious category by explaining the experiments for the general reader without losing important information by oversimplification.

Another example is in the medical aspects of relaxation. Dr. Edmund Jacobson wrote two versions of his experiments in this area. One is a technical book entitled *Progressive Relaxation: A Physiological and Clinical Investigation of Muscular States and Their Significance in Psychological and Medical Practice.* The popular version is a self-help book entitled *You Must Relax: A Practical Method of Reducing the Strains of Modern Living.* The titles alone tell the difference. The popular version concentrates on how-to-do-it, with information about the theory written in everyday language.

Experts writing in the humanities present different problems. For example, many scholars write for both specialists and the general public. Lionel Trilling, the literary critic, is an example. His book *The Liberal Imagination: Essays on Literature and Society* is scholarly, while *The Experience of Literature* is for the general reader. However, many books about literature are highly specialized, as the titles of the following show: Edward W. Rosenheim's *Swift and the Satirist's Art*, Marvin T. Herrick's *Comic Theory in the 16th Century*, Donald D. Stone's *Novelists in a Changing World: Meredith, James, and the Transformation of English Fiction in the 1880's*, and John J. Richetti's *Popular Fiction Before Richardson: Narrative Patterns 1700–1739*. On the other hand, such books as Ian Watt's *Rise of the Novel*, Percy G. Adams's *Travelers and Travel Liars: 1660–1880*, about popular travel books, and J. T. Taylor's *Early Opposition to the English Novel: Popular Reaction from 1760 to 1830* fall in the ambiguous area of "it depends."

Scholars such as Daniel J. Boorstin in American history; Erik Barnouw in broadcasting; Irving Howe, Alfred

Kazin, Elizabeth Janeway, and Joyce Carol Oates in contemporary American literature; Loren Eisley and Margaret Mead in anthropology; Isaac Asimov in science; and Konrad Lorenz in ethnology write scholarly books and articles that overlap into the serious category. Their articles appear in current issues of the serious magazines listed in the next section, and their books, while meeting all the requirements for expert writing, are read with interest by the general public.

Therefore, how useful a specific scholarly, expert, or professional publication can be to you depends upon how it is written, your interest in the subject, and sometimes, upon vocabulary. The most specialized vocabularies are in such subjects as medicine, mathematics, and all areas of science. Publications in literature, history, sociology, education, art, and other liberal arts subjects frequently require special knowledge, although many can be useful to you not only for the information provided, but also for the bibliographies. In the books, you will find the bibliographies either after each chapter or at the back of the book. In the professional journals, the references will usually come after the article. If scholars or experts are interviewed on tape or film, you can find their published works under their names in the library card catalogue or periodical index for that subject.

2. Serious

Serious publications resemble scholarly ones by presenting information in an objective, unemotional way with adequate support from experiments and experts. However, the language in serious publications is usually nontechnical and more informal than in scholarly writing. The writer—the scholar or a knowledgeable, general author—will explain ideas thoroughly and will not assume that a reference to background material that would be known to another specialist will be known to every reader. A serious publication can be widely read and become "popular" as far as sales are concerned, although not "popular" according to the definition in the next section. These publications, both books and magazine articles, will be most useful to you. They usually provide the bulk of the material for most beginning research papers. Serious books usually provide formal bibliographies for both substantiation and further reading, while the articles in serious magazines incorporate references into the text.

An example of a serious book written for the general public by a scholar is *The Ascent of Man* by J. Bronowski. The original version was written for his television documentary of the same name, and the book is a print version of the same script. Scholar Daniel J. Boorstin's articles appear in such serious magazines as *Fortune*, while articles by Alfred Kazin, Irving Howe, Elizabeth Janeway and Joyce Carol Oates appear in *Atlantic Monthly, Harper's Magazine*, the old *Saturday Review*, and the current *Saturday Review/World*. Both *Scientific American* and *Psychology Today* publish versions of studies that, while possibly appearing oversimplified and too popularized to experts, are serious and useful to general readers and research paper writers such as you. A few other serious magazines that you will find useful and easily available in your library include *American Heritage, Current History, Commentary, Commonweal, Smithsonian Magazine, New York Times Magazine, Horizon*, and *National Geographic*. These and others—as well as popular magazines, which will be defined in the next section—are indexed in the beginning researcher's best and truest friend, *The Reader's Guide to Periodical Literature.*

3. Popular

Popular publications range through a long continuum and vary widely in content. These are the most easily available books and magazines because, as the category indicates, they are written for mass audiences. It's in this category that most of your judgments have to be made.

(a) At one end of the continuum are the books, magazines, and nonprint sources such as television documentaries that resemble serious sources. In these, complex ideas are explained and their complexity recognized. The material appeals to the emotions, but does not exclude the intellect. Reference is usually made to several experts and original sources given within the article. Articles from *Esquire* and *Playboy*, for example, fall into this category, although generally these two magazines exploit male sexuality. *New York* magazine is another example from this end of the popular continuum. The articles deal with thoughtful subjects with serious intent, but fairly superficially, with sources skimmed over or ignored. *Consumer's Reports, Ebony, Holiday,* and *Ms.* are other magazine examples here. Examples of television documentaries include such series as *Nova, The Thin Edge, Survival, The Wild Kingdom,* and the Jacques Cousteau marine biology series. Examples of books include those that overlap with the serious category, such as Marshall Fishwick's *The Hero, American Style,* which is based on the study of American folklore, Michael Pearson's *Those Damned Rebels,* which is a view of the American revolution through British eyes, and the nonfiction currently on the best-seller list. *All the President's Men* by Carl Bernstein and Bob Woodward is the type of best seller at this end of the popular continuum and would be usable for a research paper about either investigative reporting or contemporary politics.

(b) In the middle of the popular continuum, covering the largest number of publications, are those that combine both acceptable and nonacceptable practices. These publications are easily available in libraries and at newsstands, but they are the ones about which you have to decide whether they are acceptable sources for your research paper. For example, most of the self-help books in psychology, such as *Creative Aggression, I'm OK, You're OK,* and *How To Be Your Own Best Friend,* are in the middle range of the popular continuum. They are based on the work of experts, although simplified, and provide sources for substantiation and further reading. The writing appeals primarily to the emotions, but there is enough factual information to make these books useful in research papers in various aspects of psychology.

Robert Ardrey's *African Genesis* and Elaine Morgan's *The Descent of Women* are both popular books about animal behavior and its relationship to humanity. Ardrey quotes scholarly sources, such as R. S. L. Leakey, Raymond S. Dart, and Konrad Lorenz, to name a few, while Morgan quotes Ardrey and other popularizers. The usefulness of books such as these must be decided according to your subject and the requirements for the paper. They could be useful to you both for their interpretations and for further bibliography.

A medical treatment that has received a great deal of publicity is hormone treatment for women, and publications about this subject span the whole continuum of the popular category. Dr. Robert Wilson, a gynecologist who had worked for over forty years in the research and application of hormone treatment, wrote a popular book called *Feminine Forever* in which the appeal was primarily to women's emotions—including the title—but the medical information was scholarly and expert. Dr. Wilson's status as an expert was firmly established in such professional publications as *Journal of the American Medical Association, Clinical Medicine,* and *Western Journal of Surgery, Obstetrics and Gynecology.* However, articles appearing in such popular magazines as *Ladies' Home Journal, McCall's,* and their sister publications were written by people who are neither experts nor science writers. Generally, when preparing their articles, these writers base their information on an interview with a physician who is a competent practitioner, but not an established authority. The magazine writers concentrate on simplifying the material and appealing to the emotions of their readers, not on presenting the full complexity of the ideas.

How do you recognize the real authority? Look for the names of the people the popular book and magazine article writers quote, then see if those persons have any printed material available. Generally a real expert will be published in his or her professional journals and have at least one serious or scholarly book on the library shelves. You can also check a professional *Who's Who* to discover the person's background. You can apply this test to most fields. Is the person quoted as a historian in a popular magazine accepted by his or her profession? The evidence is in the historical journals and the number of times his or her work is referred to in books and articles by other historians. Does the person who signs his or her name to a book review in a popular magazine have any stature among literary scholars?

The evidence is in the literary journals and the number of times that author's work is footnoted in books and articles by other literary scholars. If the names appear in your textbook in the bibliography lists at the ends of chapters or in the lists at the ends of encyclopedia articles, or you keep stumbling upon them in your reading, you know you have the real authorities on the subject.

Another way to tell the value and reliability of a source is to notice the publisher. Generally the university presses publish the works of real authorities. Major, long-established, commercial publishing firms are also fairly careful, but sometimes subordinate reputation and conscience to profit. Beware of the book published by a "vanity" press. They call their work "cooperative publication" and call themselves "subsidy presses." They feed on an unpublished writer's desire to see his or her deathless prose in print, however unsupported by evidence, however bizarre or hysterical his or her opinions might be, and no matter how many times this particular book has been rejected by reputable publishers. The vanity press requires the writers to pay for the printing costs of the book, saying that they will be reimbursed from profits, which seldom appear. If you can't decide whether or not a publication is of this type, you will find directories among the specialized reference works in which to check. Both librarians and instructors are knowledgeable about publishers.

(c) At the far end of the popular continuum are the publications that rely primarily on stirring up emotions and which give little real information. These publications oversimplify ideas, offering part for the whole without establishing the basic complexity of the ideas. They use would-be authorities, limit quotations to one or two people, and give no bibliographic sources for fact checking. For example, the majority of women's magazines, such as *Ladies' Home Journal, Mademoiselle,* and *Seventeen,* are in this end of the popular category. Their articles appeal primarily to emotion and are based on very little factual material. The facts they do give are oversimplified and superficial. Other examples are *People, Argosy, Saga, Sports Afield, In the Know, Coronet, Hot Rod,* and *Car and Driver.*

Popular books made up almost entirely of case histories, such as some books about drug use, appeal only to the emotions. They present little information, and your consideration of their use as sources for your research must be very cautious.

Among the unacceptable publications on the popular continuum are the exposé books and magazine articles that supposedly reveal, in a highly charged, emotional way, the TRUTH about almost anything or anyone temporarily in public view. The biographies and autobiographies in this category are "intimate and revealing" and the personal experiences are spiritual or psychological journeys from sin to salvation or alienation to acceptance, with much heavier emphasis on the sin or unacceptable behavior than on the salvation or psychological acceptance. The so-called facts in these publications are seldom accurate. These popular publications are not acceptable as research paper sources for most subjects. For some aspects of sociology and psychology, you possibly could make use of these overly emotional and usually superficial revelations, but check first with your instructor before including them in your paper.

News Magazines and Newspapers. News magazines and newspapers fall into a special category within the popular range. Their main work is reporting events and incidents, usually disasters. This results in a topicality and superficiality that make news publications of little value as major sources for research papers. This is particularly true of the various "think" articles printed in news publications, such as the "Ideas" essays in *Newsweek*. The reporters or editors survey the topic so quickly and write the article so rapidly that they touch important aspects of the subject superficially, usually promoting the currently popular emotional attitude indirectly. These articles cause great irritation and much teeth-gnashing among members of the professions written about because they know the public is getting incomplete information. Such articles are of limited value as sources for research papers unless your subject is one that has been reported as news, you are tracing developments in the news, or you are writing about a political subject in which newspaper editorials are useful.

Most instructors are reasonable about permitting one such source to be used in a paper, but generally think that reading five articles in *Newsweek* or *Sports Illustrated* is not adequate research. Therefore, use newspapers and news magazines with judgment, depending upon your topic and the preferences of your instructor.

To summarize the general basis upon which to judge popular publications: The mark of an acceptable popular book, magazine article, or nonprint source is appeal to the intellect, explanation of complex material with recognition of its complexity, reference to several scholars in the subject, and sources given either in the text or following it for fact checking.

The mark of an unacceptable popular book, magazine article, or nonprint source is appeal to the emotions, oversimplification of ideas, use of one or two would-be authorities, and no bibliographic material for fact checking.

Between the two extremes of popular material is the

area within which you will have to make the most judgments. This is the vast quantity of easily available material
that uses some aspects of both acceptable and unacceptable
material.

4. Exploitive

Exploitive publications—books, magazines, films, and
newspapers—are produced to stimulate the reader sexually
and emotionally. Sometimes there is an appearance of fact
interwoven with the material, sometimes revelations about
public figures even more intimate than anyone ever thought
possible are promised, but the main purpose is exploitation
of sex, pity, sentimentality, fear, and horror. The sexual
revolution of the 1960s has filled the news and magazine
stands with paperback books, magazines, and newspapers
devoted to exploitation, and hardback book publication has
also increased proportionately. A few of the magazines in
this category are *Playgirl, Penthouse, Viva, Redbook, Cos-
mopolitan, Oui,* all the confession and "true experience"
magazines, and the film and television fan magazines.
Exploitive newspapers include the *National Enquirer, National Star, National Tatler,* and *Midnight.* The books are
too numerous to name but can be identified by their
emphasis on sex and intimate revelations. These publications are not acceptable sources for research papers.

Study of the four main categories of publications will
form the basis of your judgment about which material to use
for your sources. With these categories in mind, you are
ready to search bibliographic catalogues for possibilities for
your working bibliography.

One more small hint before you begin: Note the date of

issue for periodicals and the copyright date for books and films before you make out a bibliography card. Unless you are writing a paper that requires older information, stick to material published within the last ten to fifteen years. Your chances of finding the item in the library are better. In addition, material in the older items is frequently out of date and is sometimes contradicted by newer material. It takes an expert in the subject to evaluate properly two publications separated by twenty to thirty years; therefore, use more recently published items.

Preparing Working Bibliography Cards

Prepare cards for your working bibliography from the references that follow. List, *one to each 3 × 5 index card,* possible sources of information about your topic. Follow the model bibliography card forms illustrated in the section that comes after these references.

- **Books**

Library Card Catalogue. This is "old reliable" for books in every library.
Encyclopedia Articles. Look for the list of scholarly books and articles at the end of the article.

- **Magazine and journal articles**

Reader's Guide to Periodical Literature. This is the single major source of articles in serious, popular, and a few scholarly magazines in America. It does not list books. Its stated aim is to index contents of "periodicals of a broad, general, and popular character to provide a well-balanced selection of representative scientific and subject fields." The publisher, H. W. Wilson Company, confers with the American Library Association and frequently adds and deletes entries. For example, the following magazines were added recently: *American History Illustrated, BioScience, International Wildlife, Ms., Oceans, Psychology Today,* and *Smithsonian Magazine*—all useful sources for research papers.

Specialized Indexes. These indexes cover a great variety of subjects. The magazine articles and essays from books listed range from serious to scholarly. The following is not a complete list of the specialized indexes available, but it provides guidance to their variety and depth.

1. *Art Index*—covers articles in 110 fine arts magazines and museum bulletins.
2. *Biography Index*—covers biographical material in books and magazines.
3. *Social Science and Humanities Index*—formerly called *International Index to Periodicals,* this covers articles in magazines and journals in the wide range of subjects the title suggests.
4. *Applied Science and Technology Index*—covers articles in 225 periodicals.
5. *Education Index*—covers articles in 200 magazines, journals, yearbooks, and bulletins.
6. *Essay and General Literature Index*—covers critical and analytical essays about literature and philosophical ideas in books.
7. *Library Literature Index*—covers articles in 165 magazines, journals, and any other publications where material about library management is published.
8. *Index to Periodical Articles By and About Negroes*—indexes articles from 29 serious black periodicals that are not indexed elsewhere.
9. *Cumulated Abridged Index Medicus*—indexes material from biomedical journals.

10. *Guide to Historical Literature*—published by the American Historical Association, it indexes items from serious and scholarly publications.
11. *Index of Economic Journals*—covers articles in professional economic journals.
12. *International Nursing Index*—articles from over 200 nursing journals listed by title and author.
13. *Public Affairs Information Service*—indexes material in economics and public affairs.
14. *Business Periodicals Index*—covers popular and serious articles on business topics.
15. *The Agricultural Index*—deals with popular and serious articles about agriculture.
16. *Speech Index*—a guide to the contents of collections of important speeches.
17. *The Music Index*—indexes articles in more than a hundred publications.
18. *Guide to Dance Periodicals*—basic index to dance magazines.
19. *May issue each year of PMLA (Publication of the Modern Language Association)*—indexes all articles, books, and other publications about literature and individual writers that were published during the preceding year. Indexed under subject and author written about.
20. *Index to the Little Magazines*—index to over 50 literary magazines not covered by other indexes.

• *Newspapers*

New York Times Index. Covers articles published, daily and Sunday, since 1913.
The Newspaper Index. Indexes articles in the *Chicago Tribune, Los Angeles Times, New Orleans Times-Picayune* and *Washington Post.*

The Christian Science Monitor Index.
Wall Street Journal Index.
(Note: Back issues of newspapers are usually stored on
    microfilm in a special location in the library.)

- *Government publications*

Monthly Catalog of United States Government Publications.
    Lists all the publications—books, pamphlets, periodi-
    cals—published by the United States government. An
    annual index helps you locate them readily.
Selected United States Government Publications. The most
    popular books and pamphlets are listed in this index.
Pamphlet Index of Government and Business Publications.
    Lists pamphlets published by the government and
    private industry. The government's are usually more
    objective than the ones published by individual busi-
    nesses. The latter tend to publicize themselves.

- *Nonprint sources*

Individual Library Film, Record, and Tape Catalogues.
    Because libraries now recognize that they must be
    multi-media centers, as well as depositories of print
    materials, most provide catalogues of their holdings.
    Sometimes these are incorporated into the card cata-
    logue; sometimes there are individual catalogues. In
    addition, some libraries keep in their reference rooms
    the nonprint catalogues of the nearest large metropoli-
    tan public library or long-established university library.
    The latter materials can usually be requested through
    interlibrary loan service.
Index to 16mm Educational Films. Indexed by subject and
    title.

Educator's Guide to Free Films. Available films indexed by
   subject.
Index to Educational Records. Recordings listed by subject
   headings with short description of contents of each.
Index to Educational Audio Tapes. Tapes about educational
   subjects listed according to subject.
Research in Education Index. As the title indicates.
Current Index to Journals in Education. Detailed index for
   articles in 500 education journals.
Microfiche and *microcards* are sometimes part of a library's
   nonprint resources. These are cards containing whole
   articles and/or contents of a complete issue of a
   journal or magazine. The material has been so reduced
   in size that it must be put on a magnifying machine to
   read. The cards are similar to microfilm, but contain
   more material in a smaller space.

As you investigate the catalogues and indexes appropriate to your subject, record accurately and completely all
the publishing information called for in each of the three
types of bibliography cards illustrated later in this section.
The three types are the work horses of the majority of
bibliography work. It is seldom that anything you discover
cannot find a home within one of these three types.

The three types are as follows: 1. Books, pamphlets,
films, recordings, television documentaries and specials, or
any other individual publication. 2. Articles from magazines,
journals, books of readings, anthologies, or any other item
published as part of a collection. 3. Newspapers, news
magazines, and newscasts.

These forms are based on the MLA (Modern Language
Association) Style Sheet, and nonprint sources are incorporated into the type of bibliography cards appropriate to each
kind of publication. For example, a television network

documentary about marine biology, such as those of Jacques Cousteau, is an individual publication; therefore, you write a card of the book type. The same rule applies to recordings if the whole album or tape is about the same subject. If, however, you are using only one cut from an album that contains a variety of songs—for example, for a paper about contemporary lyrics—then write a card of the article type.

It is important to record publishing information on each bibliography card according to the models that follow. Then you can accurately transfer this information into the proper footnote and bibliography page forms. Both kinds of forms will be fully described and models provided in the appropriate step; however, for a quick overview, note how it is done in the following example.

Assume that your paper is "The Impact of Advertising," and you have found needed information in a book about specific ad campaigns and their effects. Record that information on your bibliography card as follows:

```
Robert Glatzer
The New Advertising:  The Great Campaigns
from Avis to Volkswagen
New York:  Citadel Press, 1970
```

Then transpose the elements into the following footnote form:

[1] Robert Glatzer, *The New Advertising: The Great Campaigns from Avis to Volkswagen* (New York: Citadel Press, 1970), p. 50.

and later into the bibliography page form:

Glatzer, Robert. *The New Advertising: The Great Campaigns from Avis to Volkswagen.* New York: Citadel Press, 1970.

As you can see, once the information is recorded on the bibliography card in the proper order, you need change only punctuation and placement on the page to write correct footnote and bibliography page forms.

Bibliography Card Forms

Place the library call number in the upper right corner or lower left corner of each bibliography card, whichever place is more convenient for you. However, keep the location consistent throughout your work.

1. Books, pamphlets, films, recordings, television documentaries, or any other individual publication:

- **Books with one or more authors or editors**

```
Michael Pearson
Those Damned Rebels:  The American Revolution as
Seen Through British Eyes
New York:  G. P. Putnam's Sons, 1972
```

```
Oscar Cargill, N.B. Fagin, and W.J. Fisher, editors
O'Neill and His Plays
New York: New York University Press, 1961
```

(*Note:* Look at the illustration under *Article from book of readings or an anthology,* p. 46, to see how one article from this book is handled.)

- ***Pamphlet with committee or group author***

> U.S. Department of the Interior
> <u>Threatened</u> <u>Wildlife</u> <u>of</u> <u>the</u> <u>United</u> <u>States</u>
> Washington: Government Printing Office, 1973

- ***Film***

> <u>Birds</u> <u>of</u> <u>the</u> <u>Prairie</u> (Film)
> Blackhawk Film Co., 1972

- ***Filmstrip***

> <u>The</u> <u>Kingdom</u> <u>of</u> <u>the</u> <u>Forest</u> (Filmstrip)
> Lyceum Productions, 1972

- ***Tape recording***

> <u>The</u> <u>Ideal</u> <u>Teacher</u>: <u>A</u> <u>Scholarly</u> <u>Discussion</u> (Tape)
> Educational Research Group, 1970

- ***Television documentary***

> Charles Collingwood, Narrator
> <u>Picasso</u> <u>is</u> <u>90</u>
> CBS News, 1971

2. Articles from magazines, journals, books of readings, anthologies, or any other item published as part of a collection:

- *Monthly magazine*

```
William T. Keeton
"The Mystery of Pigeon Homing"
Scientific American
231 (December 1974), 96-106
  or:  December 1974, pp. 96-106
```

- *Weekly magazine—no author given*

```
"The Palestinian Tug of War"
Newsweek
4 November 1974, pp. 36-38
```

- *Weekly magazine—author given*

```
Richard Reeves
"The Senate Syndrome"
Newsweek
4 November 1974, p. 11
```

- *Professional journal*

```
Peggy Rosenthal
"Feminism and Life in Feminist Biography"
College English
36 (October 1974), 180-184
```

If the article does not have an author, start your card on the second line with the title, and go on from there.

Regarding the fourth line on the article cards: your

decision about whether to include the volume number (as illustrated in the two choices given for the Keeton article in the monthly magazine above) depends upon how the publication's pages are numbered. (Numbering pages is called *pagination*.) If, as in *Scientific American*, the page numbers start with 1 at the beginning of each issue each month, then you have a choice of the two ways to record date of issue and beginning and end page numbers of the articles. If, as in *College English* and most professional journals, the page numbers start with 1 in the first issue of the year and continue until possibly page 1256 on the last page of the last issue of the year—which makes a volume—then you are obliged to use the form containing the volume number, date of issue in parentheses, and the beginning and end page numbers without *pp.,* which stands for "pages," before them.

- **One cut from a recording**

```
Jimi Hendrix
"Third Stone From the Sun"
The Jimi Hendrix Experience
Burbank, California:  Reprise Records, 1971
```

- **One record from an album**

```
Helge Kokeritz
"Middle English"
A Thousand Years of English Pronunciation
Pleasantville, New York:  Educational Audio
Visual, 1961
Record 1, Side 2
```

• *Article from book of readings or an anthology*

```
Malcolm Cowley
"A Weekend with Eugene O'Neill"
O'Neill and His Plays
Oscar Cargill, N. B. Fagin, and W. J. Fisher, editors
New York:  New York University Press, 1961
```

3. Articles and editorials from newspapers, news magazines, and newscasts:

Most of the time, newspaper and news magazine articles will not give the author; therefore, start your card with the title. Use the headlines for the article titles, as illustrated in the next set of cards. If an article starts on one page, then jumps to another, record both pages with "and" rather than a dash between the two numbers. The dash says that the article covers all the pages between the two numbers, which, in the case of newspapers particularly, is not so.

Nationally known newspapers need not have state names added to the title for identification. Those of small towns should. For example, you need not add the state to such major newspapers as *The New York Times, The Philadelphia Bulletin, The Chicago Tribune, The Los Angeles Times,* or others of similar stature. However, such papers as the following and others similar to them need to be identified by both city and state: *The Cumberland* (Maryland) *News, The Tallahassee* (Florida) *Democrat, The Muncie* (Indiana) *Press, The Tucson* (Arizona) *Daily Citizen.*

To use material from a radio or television newscast requires a quick ear and a ready pencil because the spoken words flow by so fast. One way around this, if your paper is about contemporary events and you know something you can use will be in the broadcast, is to tape the audio to replay for either summary or direct quotation. A short summary can usually be written as the anchorperson or reporter is speaking. Note the name of the speaker, identify his or her function, note the most important words of the item as the title, and include the name of the newscast, time, and date as the publishing data.

- *Newspaper article without author*

```
"Inflation Hurts India's Middle Class"
The New York Times
15 December 1974, Sec. 1, p. 2
```

- *Newspaper article with author*

```
M. A. Farber
"Ford Foundation to Slash Grants Over Next
Four Years"
The New York Times
15 December 1974, Sec. 1, pp. 1 and 30
```

- *Newspaper editorial*

```
"Congress Takes New Look at Foreign Aid" (Editorial)
The Cumberland (Maryland) News
17 December 1974, p. 9
```

- *News magazine*

```
"The Palestinian Tug of War"
Newsweek
4 November 1974, pp. 36-38
```

- *Newscast*

```
John Chancellor, anchor
NBC Nightly News
6:30 p.m., 8 January 1975
```

```
Heather Bernard, reporter
"Bomb Explosion at La Guardia Airport"
NBC News
5 p.m., 30 December 1975
```

The foregoing bibliography card forms should be able to handle the majority of the sources in your research papers. Occasionally you might find a source with publishing data that fits none of these models or has additional information such as series numbers or volume numbers of a set. Should this happen, record all the publishing information that fits one of these models, then add whatever else you find on the next lines. If this source becomes part of your final bibliography and you cannot find an appropriate model for a footnote form among those provided under Step 10, *Writing the Paper*, ask your instructor how to handle it. For the majority of beginners' papers, however, these forms will be sufficient.

Part III

THE RESEARCH

Step 6: Finding Usable Material

After you have accumulated a large collection of possible sources in your bibliography, search out each one. Scan each to decide its value to your topic. Check the publishing information on your card against the title page of the source for accuracy if the source proves useful. The title page is *always* the final word; the bibliographic source is sometimes in error. On the cards of those items that are useless, mark the words "Useless" or "Can't Use," or something to indicate that you have seen and evaluated the item. Mark the others "Read" or "Useful" or some similar word. At the end of this phase, separate the cards, but do not discard the useless ones. Sometime during your reading they might be referred to, and you very easily could forget that you had already looked at that item.

Read all the useful sources and take notes from them.

Isn't it ironic that the major, most time-consuming, hardest, and most important part of this project can be stated in one sentence, while several pages are needed to cover mechanical details such as footnote forms? Add the inspirational thought, "Be sure to record everything that you can use in your paper," and we are ready to deal with the major problems of deciding what to put into your notes and how it should be put there.

The material that you excerpt from your sources will depend upon the point you are going to make in your paper. It is impossible for any teacher, however talented, to pinpoint specific and exact "how-to-do-it" instructions because there are too many variables, ranging from topic to individual perception. However, pointers are available from the illustrations in this book. For example, to show a mechanical method of excerpting notes from the article "The Hectic Life of the Alpha Bull" that follows, content had to be shown also. The material under the item "When to use each note-taking method" is a guide also for what kinds of ideas and substance to excerpt from your sources.

Step 7: Taking Notes

A. Materials

A great deal of mythology surrounds the use of note cards; however, these are tools: a means to an end, not the end itself. Note cards are a convenience, not a necessity—unless a specific instructor makes them so. Some students write extraordinarily fine papers by taking notes in stenographer's pads. Others write inadequate papers after filling five 100-card packages with notes. It is not the kind of paper on which you write your notes that is important, but the material that you choose and the kind of thought that goes into that choice. If your instructor requires a certain kind of note card, by all means use it. If you have your choice, use anything that is comfortable and convenient. Be consistent, though. Don't start with 6 × 8 cards, use a few sheets from a spiral notebook, some 3 × 5 cards, and so on. You'll have a mess on your hands when you write your paper. Pick one type of material for your notes, then stay with it.

B. Identifying Your Notes

There should be a bibliography card for each set of notes. Key the notes to the card in one of the following ways:

1. Letter the bibliography card, then place the letter and a number on each note card or page of notes.

- *Bibliography card*

```
Burney J. LeBoeuf
"The Hectic Life of the Alpha Bull"
Psychology Today
October 1974, pp. 104-108
```

- *Note cards or pages*

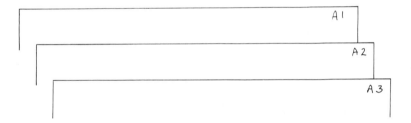

2. Place the author's last name in the upper right hand corner of each note card or page of notes together with the appropriate card or page number. This can become confusing only if you happen to use two sources by the same author. In that case, add the title after the author's name to keep each source fully identified.

- *Bibliography card*

```
Marshall Fishwick
The Hero, American Style
New York:  David McKay Company, 1969
```

- *Note cards or pages*

When you have an article without the author's name, use the title for your key. If the title is very long, use a short, clear, two or three word version.

- *Bibliography card*

```
"Inflation Hurts India's Middle Class"
The New York Times
15 December 1974, Sec. 1, p. 2
```

- *Note cards or pages*

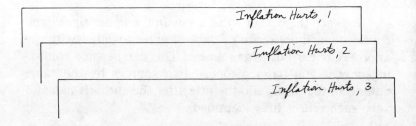

C. Methods of Taking Notes

Knowledge of several methods of note taking is useful when reading material for your paper. Each method is appropriate for different purposes, but, ultimately, you will use combinations of all. Therefore, it's important to be able to switch from one type to another as you are reading. The three basic methods are as follows:

1. Summary— a short statement of the author's main idea in your own words. This will be shorter than the original.

2. Paraphrase—a complete restatement of all the author's ideas and all the supportive evidence presented in your own words. This will parallel the original and, therefore, will be either the same length or longer.

(*Note*: Of these two methods of note taking, summary is used more often.)

3. Direct quotation—word-for-word, punctuation-mark-for-punctuation-mark copy of significant and important statements from the original.

In the first two kinds of note taking, it's all right to change the order or organization of the author's presentation, as long as you don't change the meaning. In the third type, nothing should be changed. As you read through your sources, you will utilize both summary and paraphrase, as well as direct quotation of key phrases, sentences, and paragraphs of significance. Direct quotations should always be of key ideas and/or pungently worded phrases and sentences, typical of the author's style. If the material is not significant and/or individually styled so that any change would dilute the meaning or ruin the author's writing, use summary to excerpt the main idea.

If an idea of your own or an objection to the material is triggered as you are reading and taking notes, include your comments in your notes in parentheses or brackets and/or different colored ink. This commentary is important to your paper, but it is also important that it not be mixed up with the material from your source. Your spontaneous commentary contributes to your individual statement; however, you must accurately record the information from your source and indicate which material is whose.

To illustrate how to take notes from sources, we will use an excerpt from a magazine article and follow the procedure through from bibliography card to note card or page. The model will help you understand both how to take notes and how to key them from bibliography cards to notes. None of the sources that you will use for your paper will be as short as this. This is just a piece of the original; however, the same principles apply to longer works. Also, you will probably handwrite your notes, but these illustrations are typed for easier reading.

This article was used as part of the information collected for a paper about animal behavior. Read the article through first, then compare the notes with it.

- *Bibliography card*

```
Burney J. LeBoeuf
"The Hectic Life of the Alpha Bull"
Psychology Today
October 1974, pp. 104-108
```

- *Note card or page*

```
How alpha bull achieves dominance:                    A I

p.104: The Northern elephant seal alpha bull spends the
       weeks at the mating ground (rookery) before arrival
       of females bluffing or fighting other males to
       establish dominance.

       "Only the males who are the best fighters earn a
       high enough position in elephant-seal society to get
       close to females."
```

The Hectic Life
of the Alpha Bull

Burney J. LeBoeuf

[Following from p. 104]

When men who fight reluctantly find themselves in a tight spot, they quickly declare their proclivity: "I'm a lover, not a fighter!" The Northern elephant seal has no such choice. If he's not a fighter, he'll never be a lover. Only the males who are the best fighters earn a high enough position in elephant-seal society to get close to females. They provide a lucid example of the Darwinian struggle for existence.

The contest begins each December when Northern elephant seals haul out of the water on small islands off the coast of California and Baja California, Mexico. Males arrive at the mating ground about two weeks before the females come ashore in late December or early January.

The exact time that a male arrives at the rookery is critical. If he arrives too early, he may have to fight too long to earn and maintain high social status. He may become so exhausted by the time the females are in heat, that another bull can easily depose him before he gets a chance to mate. If he arrives later than most of the other males, he may have to fight too hard to break down the already established social hierarchy. A smart bull arrives at the rookery rather early, secures a rank as one of the top five males, and then rests as much as he can until the females are ready.

When the big bulls, who are about 16 feet long and weigh over three tons, lumber ashore in early December, the bloody battles begin. Initially, one bull tries to dominate another by bluffing. He lifts his head, issuing a series of loud, low-pitched guttural blasts. When his threats are ineffective, he attacks. He rears back, lunges at his adversary with the upper part of his body, and bites his foe with his long, sharp canines. The blows are so powerful that the blubbery exterior of the adversary undulates from the impact. Some of these donnybrooks last for three quarters of an hour, and blood colors the water for yards around. The loser always signals defeat by retreating, and the next time the two meet he moves out of the dominant bull's way. The sum of these individual displacements results in a strict social hierarchy.

[Following from p. 106]

Almost all the bulls bear assorted wounds and scars throughout the three-month breeding season. Some have punctured eyeballs; others have split snouts or chunks of skin or blubber torn from their backs. The scars accumulate year after year, but battle injuries are rarely fatal.

The top male, or alpha bull, dominates all others. He is completely free to move anywhere, to do whatever he wants. The second ranking bull defers to the alpha, but dominates all others. Moving down the social hierarchy, each bull has one more superior to avoid and one less subordinate to dominate.

Fight a Tired Alpha. When the females arrive at the rookery, the males have established their pecking order, and to the victors go the spoils. The alpha male plants himself in the center of the group of cows, and treats it as his harem. Other males get as close to the females as rank permits. The alpha male maintains his position by repelling any intruder. Usually, threats alone suffice, but there are times when he must fight. A smart strategy for an upward-climbing bull is to challenge a tired alpha immediately after he has had a fight. It doesn't matter when or how the alpha male loses a fight. Once he has, his vulnerability is exposed and his bluffs no longer work. He plummets down the social hierarchy, out of serious contention for access to the cows. In the rookery we have observed on Año Nuevo Island off Northern California, deposed dictators usually go into exile on the mainland a half-mile away.

Six days after a female arrives at the rookery and joins a harem, she gives birth to a pup conceived the previous year; she nurses it for four weeks. In late January, she comes into heat and she mates during the last four or five days of nursing. She copulates several times each day, and finally returns to the ocean, slimmer than when she came ashore, but pregnant again, probably by the alpha male.

Temporary Residents. Males fight frequently and intensely when females start to come into heat. This is when rank pays off, and there is a mighty scramble to defeat superiors and achieve a higher social position. For the alpha bull, this period is particularly precarious. If he survives all challenges during this week, he usually remains in charge of the harem, and the impregnation of the females in it, throughout the rest of the season.

```
        Method of bluffing:  ". . .issuing a series of loud,
        low-pitched guttural blasts."

        Method of attack:  lunging at other male and biting
        into blubber on upper part of body.  Fights can last
        for almost an hour.

        Signaling defeat:  loser retreats.

        "The sum of these individual displacements results in
        a strict social hierarchy."
```

You will see in the notes that two key ideas, each a sentence long, are direct quotations. Part of a significant sentence is also quoted because the language is typical of the author's style of writing. General information is summarized.

If this material were put on note cards, you would divide the summary and direct quotations into two cards. If it were put on notebook or typewriter paper, then these notes and the ones to follow from page 106 would be on the same page.

Note the placement of the page number from the original source. It is placed in the left margin and the material indented so that, when you are using this material in your paper, you will not have to search through the notes for the page number. It is clear, accurate, easily seen, and available for placement in the footnote form without confusion, distraction, or possibility of error while you search for it in the notes.

- **Note card or page**

```
Male behavior:                                        A 2

p. 106: "Males fight frequently and intensely when females
        start to come into heat.  This is when rank pays
        off, and there is a mighty scramble to defeat
        superiors and achieve a higher social position."
```

> Alpha males achieve their rank before females ar-
> rive. After females arrive, alphas must defend
> rank by keeping other males away from their harem.

Note that the two-sentence direct quotation of significant information has been moved from its original position
in the article. This does not change the author's meaning. It
just puts the key idea in an easily accessible location.

If you use the alternative keying method, that of
placing the author's name on the notes, substitute "Le-
Boeuf" for the letter "A."

As you can see, good note taking is not writing
everything down. It is selective. It is recording the main
ideas and supporting evidence, but discarding information
that is not appropriate to your topic. The information about
female behavior in this article was not appropriate to the
topic; therefore, it was not included in the notes.

Whether you use cards in the traditional way or sheets
of notebook paper for your notes, the orderliness in which
you record the material will be a great help in the final
writing of the paper.

D. When to Use Each Note-taking Method

Use summary and paraphrase for the following purposes:

1. For general explanation
2. To give background information
3. To tell events in history
4. To tell how historical events came about

5. To give the main ideas of a group of people holding the same viewpoint; i.e., to summarize a school of thought

6. To tell briefly the necessary plot of novels, short stories, plays, or line of thought of a poem

7. To give contributory information that is of secondary importance

Use direct quotations for the following purposes:

1. To give an important, significant, or key thought by an authority

2. To give a thought, comment, or illustration that is so well expressed or expressed in such an individual manner that to summarize would lose the flavor or individuality

3. To give a dissenting opinion by a reputable person opposing the majority

4. To give the exact words of a document of law

5. To give unusual or bizarre ideas, opinions, or comments

6. To give any ideas in conflict with the point that your paper is making that do not fit under a summary

7. To give specialized or technical information such as statistics

E. Plagiarism

This is a good place to define and illustrate plagiarism because it is during note taking that innocent and conscientious people can accidentally plagiarize.

Plagiarism is intellectual theft. Whether someone copies from a source without acknowledging the original author's work, uses or buys another person's paper, has the English major down the hall or someone else correct and rewrite a rough draft, that person is passing off another's intellect and writing ability as his or her own.

Generally, instructors can spot plagiarism because of the contrast between a student's nonprofessional writing and the polished, sophisticated sentence structure and complex vocabulary of the scholar or professional writer. How an instructor handles the situation usually depends both upon school policy and the kind of plagiarism it is.

The two main kinds of plagiarism are as follows:

1. Conscious plagiarism. This is outright copying from a published source, buying a prepared paper, using someone else's paper, or having someone rewrite a rough draft. The student who does this is completely conscious of his or her theft. Usually the student who resorts to conscious plagiarism is doing so as an act of desperation in order to salvage a grade. He or she is to be pitied, but the consequences are the same. That student has performed an act of conscious theft.

2. Unconscious plagiarism. This is an accident, generally the result of ignorance. The person who unconsciously plagiarizes usually does not fully understand how to summarize or how to insert material from his or her sources into the paper. If you will read the examples that follow and study the explanation, you will have a clear idea of both plagiarism and how to avoid it.

The illustrations on pages 64–67 consist of a page from a research paper contrasting television news writing with newspaper reporting and the text from two pages of a source for that paper, a book entitled *Television News* by Irving E. Fang. The plagiarized material is marked with numbers matched in the source. Material was copied word-for the Dow Jones Wire."[2]

Television news writing is not newspaper writing read aloud. Television news differs in content, arrangement, style and delivery. The receiver of the information is different also, although in many cases, the television news viewer is also a daily newspaper reader. He is different because the medium of television requires different degrees of attention and participation than does the medium of print. The reader must concentrate. Quite opposite demands are made on the television viewer. Using imagination, a person who watches television doesn't have to go to the news. The news comes to him. It follows him into the kitchen when he goes for a snack until he is out of earshot. The viewer doesn't have to have his full attention upon the television news. His mind may wander. The newspaper reader is not likely to be doing much else while he is reading that occupies his attention. The television news writer who offers the audience nothing but newspaper news read aloud will not keep his audience tuned in for very long.

> A 15-minute television newscast gives the audience approximately the same number of stories as does a newspaper front page and a local news page at a depth of one to three paragraphs. For a 30-minute newscast, add page 3 of the newspaper and a few more paragraphs of depth from the front page. That's all.[3]

It has been repeated that television news will never replace newspapers. Television news cannot provide the number of facts a newspaper provides. Actually television newsmen should not try. The viewer would not absorb that much detail, and would soon grow bored.

---

[2]Irving E. Fang, <u>Television News</u> (New York: Hastings House, 1968), pp. 37-38.

[3]Fang, p. 69.

64

Television News
as News

IS TELEVISION NEWS fundamentally different from newspaper news? If we strip format and technique away, are they not just the same? Certainly, any lively discussion of the merits of television news raises comparisons with the printed medium.

The answers are not simple. Fundamental differences *do* exist because of the fundamental differences between Man as Reader and Man as Listener. Yet the similarities are just as fundamental, because Reader and Listener are frequently the same person, whose interests, desire to comprehend and standards of taste are indivisible in terms of differences in media.

TELEVISION NEWS VS. NEWSPAPER NEWS

① Television news writing is not newspaper writing read aloud. Television news differs from newspaper news in content, arrangement, style and delivery. The receiver of the information is different also, although in many cases, the television news viewer is also a daily newspaper reader. He is different because the medium of television requires different degrees of attention and participation than does the medium of print. Print is a medium in which the reader must be actively involved to get the message. The reader must concentrate. He must focus his attention on the printed word, and he must let his imagination, his mind's eye, fill in the picture the text describes.

65

Quite opposite demands are made by the television medium. The viewer sits passively. He doesn't come to the news, as he would by picking up the evening paper. The news comes to him. It follows him around the room if he gets up from his chair. It follows him into the kitchen when he goes for a snack, until he is out of earshot. While he watches the tube, his sense of sight is captured, so his imagination is not called forth. However, television news does not demand the viewer's full attention. His mind may wander. The newspaper reader is not likely to be doing much else while he is reading that occupies his attention, but when he watches the news on television, he may also be carrying on a conversation, building a model airplane, or even glancing through a magazine, depending upon his degree of interest at any moment.

What this means is that the television news writer has a more elusive target at which to aim his information than does the newspaper writer. The television news writer who offers the audience nothing but newspaper news read aloud will not keep his audience tuned in for very long.

A 15-minute television newscast gives the audience approximately the same number of stories as does a newspaper front page and a local news page at a depth of one to three paragraphs. For a 30-minute newscast, add page 3 of the newspaper, and a few more paragraphs of depth from the front page. That's all.

It has been repeated often that television news will never replace newspapers. Television news, and radio news as well, cannot provide the number of facts a newspaper provides. Actually, television newsmen should not try. The viewer would not absorb that much detail, and would soon grow bored.

Let us consider what a newspaper tells its readers.

A story about a day's fighting in a distant war goes into considerable factual detail. We learn the identity of the battalion and the number of jungle miles it pierced that day and how far it is from some city we use as a reference point and how many enemy soldiers it encountered, how many it killed as against its own losses. We learn who the officer is who gives us this information, and what he has to say about the battle and the battle which is likely to follow. The story gives us similar information about the activities of a regiment a certain number of miles (we are told how many) away (we are told which direction). The same story also tells us about the day's bombing, which means learning how many bombers left from where to what targets to drop how many tons of explosives how far from what referent points, and to what degree of success according to what Air Force source. The same story may also tell us of the day's political activities in that distant country, the internal maneuverings, the attempts to control or the attempts to get out from under. We learn the names and titles and assignments of the visiting political officials and where they are going and who is meeting them and how long they intend to remain, and what they say about what they have seen so far.

for-word without citing the source, or was changed so little that it might just as well have been word-for-word.

This is obviously a case of unconscious plagiarism. If it were not, the student would not have cited the source nor made even minimal changes. Plagiarism could have been avoided by increasing the number of direct quotations and summarizing part of the information. However, this student was confused about the amount of rewriting that summary needs and about how to manipulate quotations to contribute to her own statement. In addition, she did not recognize as Fang's individual style the concrete images of the television viewer going to the kitchen and, in the same paragraph, doing a variety of other activities.

Rewriting sufficient for summary or paraphrase requires much more change than just dropping out a few words, such as "from newspaper news," in the second sentence in the paragraph marked 1 in the source, and "and radio news as well," in the paragraph marked 3.

Paragraph 1 could have been handled in either of the two following ways. The first example shows manipulation of the material in the order that Fang wrote it; the second, by changing the order.

• *Example 1*

"Television news writing is not newspaper writing read aloud. . . . [It] differs in content, arrangement, style and delivery."[3] These changes are made because a different kind of concentration is required from the television news viewer than from the newspaper reader.[4]

You can see how the information in Fang's book has been condensed and manipulated to contribute to the point the student wanted to make in her paper. The first sentence in the direct quotation is retained because it is terse and vivid, but the next sentence contained a key idea. It, therefore, had to be cut down to avoid repetition. This was done by using ellipsis, the three dots that show words have been omitted, and by adding a bracketed short pronoun-substitute for the subject to keep the meaning clear. True, some words are used in common. It's impossible to avoid that and still deal with the same subject, but the material must be condensed and wording and sentence structure substantially changed without changing the meaning.

- *Example 2*

> A different kind of writing is used in television news because of the different kind of concentration required from the television news viewer than from the newspaper reader. "Television news writing is not newspaper writing read aloud." [3]

In the next paragraph, the changes in "content, arrangement, style and delivery" should be fully explained.

The rest of the material plagiarized from Fang's book should have been handled with the same balance of direct quotations and summarized material, making sure that Fang's individual style and concrete examples are credited to him.

To avoid unconscious plagiarism, therefore, make sure you rewrite fully for summary and paraphrase, changing the organization of the source as necessary to manipulate the material for your own purposes. It is a good rule of thumb to consider concrete examples and terse, vivid phraseology as the author's individual style and use those sentences for direct quotations.

Part IV

THE WRITING

Step 8: Restatement of Subject

After you have read and taken notes from your sources, stop and reconsider what you are doing. Look at the statement you made in Step 3. Is it still possible to make that point with the material you have gathered? Will you have to shift or change the controlling idea? Decide by asking yourself, "Can I make the original point with this material?" If, because of availability of source material, the answer is no, rewrite the statement. Generally, the shifts are in emphasis, not from subject to subject. If it is necessary to change subjects, discuss the change with your instructor.

Step 9: Writing the Paper

By this time, you have read and thought so much about the material that a mental digestive process has taken place. You have made the material your own, and you are now ready to make your individual statement. Very rarely does anyone reach this moment in a research paper assignment with a topic and notes, but no idea what to do next. Because of your investigation, you are full of ideas about your subject and have evidence to support the point you want to make. You also have a concept of the form the paper will take, although you may not realize it. This concept grew partly from interest in your own topic and partly from reading mature examples of the same kind of writing by experts. In every source that you have read, you found an introduction, a body, and a conclusion, as well as molding and manipulation of sources to contribute to those authors' purposes. Now you are going to do the same.

To reinforce consciously your concept of the paper's

form, look at the model papers in this book. These are the work of students just like you who went through the same procedure. Note how they manipulated their sources, dominating, molding, and rearranging them to contribute to the purpose of the papers without changing meaning. In each paper, the student made a personal statement of opinion, yet the writing is impersonal. Note particularly how they made transitions and how the writing was handled to produce a smooth-flowing, unified paper built upon the three-block structure of introduction, body, and conclusion. The functions of each block of this structure are as follows:

- ### *Introduction*

The introduction performs three functions. It acts as an attention-getter, it fully identifies your topic, and it states the point you want to make. With the topic and point stated, you have established a contract with the reader to provide evidence to support, illustrate, and/or prove that point. The written and rewritten statement of the point you want to make that you worked on from the start of your investigation is your springboard into the introduction.

- ### *Body*

The body sets out all the evidence that you have collected from your sources to support, illustrate, and/or prove your point. The sections that follow provide directions about the mechanics of inserting quoted, summarized, and paraphrased material. The reasons listed on pages 61–62 under *When to use each note-taking method* provide a guide for the use of your source material. Keep your main point before the reader at all times, remembering that you want him or her to finish the paper agreeing with that point.

- *Conclusion*

The conclusion echoes the introduction. You say, in effect, that you have provided evidence of sufficient weight and logic of sufficient clarity to establish the point you undertook to make.

The following sections provide instructions about inserting material into your paper from your sources and illustrate the mechanics of doing so according to accepted conventions for this kind of writing. Read through all the instructions before you start to write. You will see the general dimensions of the paper, and you can locate specific, detailed instructions when you need them.

A. Working Outline

Read over the notes you have taken with the statement from Step 8 before you. Then list the major sections or divisions of your subject on a piece of paper, leaving space between each. Go back over your notes and insert, in an informal way, the support or evidence that falls under each major section. This is a rough, working outline. One page is usually more than enough. Keep it before you while you are writing the paper. It will prevent you from wandering off the subject.

The following examples are the working outlines from which the two model research papers in the back of this book were written.

- *Example 1*

                    The Influences on the Music of
                      Francis Vincent Zappa, Jr.
1. Adolescent influence—1953–58
        Rock and blues
        Otis and Thornton
2. Edgard Varèse
        Sound experiments
        Zappa's albums
3. Igor Stravinsky
        Dissonance
        Traditional orchestration
        Lumpy Gravy
        200 Motels
4. Anton Webern
        12 tone system
5. Zappa's satire
        "Flower Punk"

- *Example 2*

            Clarissa and Lovelace: The Problems of an
                    Eighteen-Year-Old Girl
1. Novel's emphasis defined
        "Protection" key
        Social examination and warning emphasis
2. Legal status of girl in 18th century
        No control of person, fortune, or life
        No protective laws for women
        1753 first civil marriage law
3. Clarissa's personal attitudes
        Poised, secure, playful at home
        Confidence crumbling re: Mr. Solmes
        Panic and flight

4. Clarissa's attitudes toward Lovelace
   Attraction and control
   Control slipping
   Confidence in him shattered
   Fear and hatred grow
   Terror and revulsion
   Regret and pity

Compare the outlines with the final versions of the papers, and you will see the value of the outline as a writing guide. Some instructors require outlines to be submitted as part of the paper; others do not. However, the outline is most valuable when it is written before the paper, not after.

B. The Rough Draft

Because of the press of time, students frequently consider writing a rough draft optional, and instructors get rough drafts instead of finished pieces of writing. Plan your work so that you will have time to write this preliminary version. Doing so refines your thinking and prevents the careless errors of hasty, unrevised writing.

Develop the rough draft from your working outline by enlarging each section into paragraphs. Write out your ideas freely and rapidly. Get everything on paper with all the vigor and punch you can put into it. Later you can tone it down if it's overwritten.

Put the rough draft aside for at least a day; more if you have time. Then read it aloud either to yourself or to someone else. Inconsistencies, grammatical errors, lack of proper cause and effect, lack of proper transitions, lack of relationship—if these are there—will be apparent and your revision can start. If you read the paper to someone else, his or her reactions and your discussion are great helps in the revision.

C. Amount of Quoted and Summarized Material

When writing your paper, balance the number of times you use direct quotations and summary or paraphrase. Don't use all of one kind. Try to end with approximately the same number of each.

D. How to Insert Direct Quotations

Direct quotations can be short, medium, or long. Both short and medium lengths are incorporated smoothly into your sentences and paragraphs, but are identified as another's writing by quotation marks. The long quotation is blocked and single-spaced in the middle of the page, *without quotation marks.* Because of its appearance, set off from the text of the paper, the material declares itself a direct quotation.

You must tell where all direct quotations come from. You do this by placing a footnote number at the end of each quotation, as illustrated in the following section. The number is repeated at the beginning of the footnote, which is placed either at the bottom of the page or on a separate footnote page at the end of the paper. The footnote itself, set up in a traditional form illustrated in Section F (page 89), shows the source of the quotation.

The following examples illustrate how to handle each length.

• *Short quotations*

A short quotation consists of a few words, such as a phrase typical of a writer's style, or part of a sentence containing key information or an important idea. The following excerpt, illustrating the use of three short quotations, is from a paper entitled "The Effect of Gin on 18th Century London." Note that the sentences containing the short quotations are written as complete, smoothly blended units. One short quotation was blended in at the end of a sentence, another in the middle, and the third at the end. It is also permissible to start sentences with short quotations. There is no rule about placement in the sentence as long as the quoted matter is properly blended and correctly identified.

Gin consumption rose "from half a million gallons in 1690 to nearly five million gallons in 1729."[8] Defoe records that, while cheap spirits were sold "as addenda to other trades, by the chandlers, grocers, inn-keepers, and the like,"[9] there were also, in the streets of London "a prodigious number of shop-keepers whose business is wholely and solely the selling of spirits and strong waters."[10]

• *Medium-sized quotations*

A medium-sized quotation consists of one or two sentences that can be incorporated into your own paragraph. Occasionally, three short sentences could be treated as a medium-sized quotation, but anything longer should be handled as a long quotation. The medium-sized quotation can be used at the beginning, middle, or end of your own paragraph.

The following illustration is from a paper entitled "Narcotic Addiction." It shows incorporation of one sentence into a paragraph:

> Before the Harrison Act and other acts were passed, most drugs were easily accessible. During World War I, one in every 1,500 was rejected from service because of addiction. In World War II, the Armed Forces reported, "One man in 10,000 selective service registrants was rejected primarily because of drug addiction."[3]

The following excerpt, from a paper about "Building the Pyramids," illustrates the insertion of a two-sentence medium-sized quotation. Although it is at the end of the paragraph, this placement is not a requirement.

> The monuments of the Old Empire belong to engineering rather than to architecture but, with all their simplicity, possess great material grandeur. They are almost wholly sepulchral, consisting of pyramids, mastabas or masonry tombs, and hypogea or excavated tombs. "There was no dynamite for blasting the rock. Human energy was the only dynamite and the machinery of the ancient world was living machinery."[5]

• *Long quotations*

The minimum length of a long quotation is approximately fifty words. This usually works out to four sentences of average length or three exceptionally long ones. There is no maximum length for long quotations; however, quotations taking up more than about one-third of a page are usually considered too long. Part of that material should be summarized or the quotation split into several sections with explanations and transitions between.

The following illustration is from a paper entitled "Aspects of Everyday Life in 17th Century England." Note how the quotation stands out between the two paragraphs of narration. Because of this, quotation marks are not needed for identification at the beginning and end. The phrase within brackets is a piece of information added by the writer for clarity. This can be done in any size quotation, if necessary for the sense of the material or to cut out unnecessary repetition. Such a device, however, should be used sparingly.

> When Charles II was restored to the throne of England in 1660, cosmetics became popular again after having been outlawed for 40 years by the Puritans. Men and women both used cosmetics. It did not matter what class they were in, servants or titled people or commoners. Cosmetics became such a menace that a bill was introduced in Parliament to protect men from women's use of them. The bill provided:
>
> > That all women, of whatever rank, profession or degree, whether virgins, maids or widows, that

> shall from and after [the date of] this Act, impose
> upon, seduce or betray into matrimony any of His
> Majesty's subjects by the scents, paints, cosmetic
> washes, artificial teeth, false hair, Spanish wool,
> iron stays, hoops, high-heeled shoes and bolstered
> hips, shall incur the penalty of the law now in
> force against witchcraft, and that the marriage
> shall be null and void.[8]

Parliament would not pass the bill because too many

of the men's wives complained. In time the uproar about

the use of cosmetics quieted, and people again became

used to them.

• *Poetry quotations*

Direct quotations from poems should be handled the same way as other quotations, depending on the amount of the poem used. If the amount is short or medium, indicate the end of the poetic line by a slash mark, using quotation marks at beginning and end. If the quotation is long, reproduce the poetic lines as you find them in your source.

The following is an example of a short poetry quotation incorporated into a sentence:

> As Poe said, "Hear the tolling of the bells,/
>
> Iron bells!/ What a world of solemn thought their
>
> monody compels!. . ."[2] In this poem he was trying to say

The following is an example of a long poetry quotation with unusual line arrangements. You will note that, as in quoted prose, quotation marks are used in short and medium length poetry quotations, but not in long ones. The three dots following the period after "block" indicate that the quotation stopped before the end of the poem.

> in the following lines of Marianne Moore's poem
>
> "To A Steam Roller," which are typical of her pattern
>
> of imagery.
>
> The illustration
> is nothing to you without the application.
>   You lack half wit. You crush all the particles down
>   into close conformity, and then walk back and
>   forth on them.
>
> Sparkling chips of rock   4
> are crushed down to the level of the parent block. . .

• *Omissions in direct quotations*

Ellipsis points, the three dots that show words have been omitted, can be used to omit unnecessary or repetitious words from a direct quotation of any length. Four dots, one of them a period, should be used if your omission starts after the end of a sentence. Your omission should not warp the author's sentence nor destroy his or her meaning. By using an ellipsis, you are adapting the source to your own purposes by reducing length, not changing meaning. The following examples show proper use of ellipses in prose quotations:

> Other references include numerous pamphlets pub-
>
> lished after 1712, including one entitled <u>Ox</u> <u>and</u> <u>Bull</u>,
>
> "an obvious play on the names . . . of Oxford and Boling-
>
> broke."9

> His humanity exhibits ". . . contemporary history com-
>
> bined with an effort to get at a timeless theme--the
>
> indestructability of the human spirit."8 This is Hersey's

> At any rate, contemporaries, who knew
> the facts, could hardly have failed to
> recognize the play on names. . . . <u>The</u>
> <u>History</u> <u>of</u> <u>John</u> <u>Bull</u> is a defense of

In poetry quotations, ellipses should be used in the same way in quotations of all lengths if only a word or two is omitted from a line. However, in long quotations, if a whole line or several are omitted, the dots should have a line to themselves, as the following illustration shows:

> In "Song of Myself," Whitman said,
>
> I am the poet of the Body and I am the poet of the Soul,
> . . .
> I am the poet of the woman the same as the man,
> And I say it is as great to be a woman as to be a man,

• *Additions to direct quotations*

Additions to direct quotations should be used only when an immediate explanation is necessary for the reader to understand the quoted material or when a short word, such as a pronoun, is substituted for several repetitious words. Enclose the addition in brackets as illustrated in the following examples. Don't use a bracketed insertion for commentary about the material, only for a needed explanation or substitution.

> "Cooper tells of the death of Bumppo [in <u>The</u> <u>Prairie</u>]
> with heart wrenching details that had his nineteenth
> century readers in tears."[5]

> It is simply incredible that, because ivory is
> required for ornaments or billiard games, the
> rich heart of Africa should be laid waste at

> this late year [1887] of the nineteenth century,
> signalized as it has been by so much advance,
> that populations, tribes and nations should be
> utterly destroyed. Whom after all does this
> bloodly seizure of ivory enrich? Only a few
> dozens of half-castes.[9]

> "Television news writing is not newspaper writing
>
> read aloud. . . . [It] differs in content, arrangement,
>
> style and delivery."[3] These changes are made because

E. How to Insert Summarized or Paraphrased Material

In appearance, summarized or paraphrased material looks like paragraphs of narrative writing. However, at the end of each section of summarized or paraphrased material, you must place a footnote number and show in the footnotes what source this material came from in the same way as for direct quotations.

The following illustration, a short section from a paper entitled "John Hersey's Novels," shows use of two summaries and a short direct quotation:

> All of his works, from A Bell for Adano to White
>
> Lotus, are touched by his almost fanatical love of man-
>
> kind. His essential belief in human good conflicts in
>
> all his novels with his portrayal of his characters.[7]
>
> ———————
>
> [7]Maxwell Geismar, American Moderns--From Rebel-
> lion to Conformity (New York: Hill and Wang, 1958),
> p. 184.

In <u>The Wall</u>, Hersey is again unable to portray any true evil, particularly the Nazi liquidation of European Jewry. His humanity exhibits ". . . contemporary history combined with an effort to get at a timeless theme--the indestructability of the human spirit."[8] This theme is found in all of Hersey's novels, especially <u>The War Lover</u>.[9]

In <u>Hiroshima</u>, Hersey is again concerned with a moral crusade, this time against the horror of the atomic bomb.

---

[8]Chester E. Eisinger, <u>Fiction of the Forties</u> (Chicago: The University of Chicago Press, 1963), p. 52.

[9]Sanders, p. 95.

F. Footnotes

1. Purpose

The academic trend today is toward simplification of footnote use and form. As you saw in the preceding illustrations for inserting material into your paper, footnotes are used mainly to tell the sources of the information from which you fashion your individual statement. In the past, footnotes have served a variety of functions, such as presenting additional commentary and explanation, providing a battleground for arguments between scholars, pointing out discrepancies in other works, and, sometimes, supplying the place where the only original idea in hundreds of pages is expressed. The last practice used to be considered scholarly modesty. However, the current opinion is that, if the material is not appropriate for the main body of the paper, it should not be used at all. It's becoming increasingly rare in scholarly publications to find commentary or argument in the footnotes, and only occasionally will a writer find it necessary to place additional information there in order not to interrupt the flow of the narrative. The writer's major purpose for using footnotes, therefore, is to inform the reader from what sources the summaries, paraphrases, and direct quotations were taken.

As a reader, when you were doing your research, you discovered other purposes for footnotes. You discovered that they are not read casually, but studiously because they provide a whole body of information and opinion that gives you insight into your subject. This is a major function of providing footnote information for all interested readers. When the reader is also your instructor, responsible for furthering your education, he or she has another objective for reading footnotes. It is evaluative, to decide whether or not you have chosen wisely among authorities in the subject, to check the accuracy of your material and your forms.

2. Placement

Numbers. The best instruction for placement of footnote numbers is illustration. Look back to the preceding section about insertion of material into your paper. In the excerpt from the paper entitled "John Hersey's Novels," placement of footnote numbers is in the text after both summarized and quoted material and before the footnotes themselves at the bottom of the page. Each number is half a space above the typing line, and for each footnote number in the text there is a matching number before the footnote itself.

Please note, also, that there are no special markings, such as periods, circles, dashes, underlines, or different colored ink, to make the footnote numbers stand out. They stand out just by being where they are supposed to be.

Footnote numbers in a paper start with [1] for the first use and continue in numerical sequence until the end of the paper whether they run to [10] or [110].

Location. There are three acceptable places for the footnotes themselves. They are as follows:

1. At the foot of the page on which the material appears. This is the traditional place and the reason for the name itself.

2. Listed on a separate page at the end of the text of the paper.

3. Keyed to the list of sources on the bibliography page. This is called "scientific notation."

Placing footnotes at the bottom of each page is the best known and most traditional way to handle them. It is advantageous for the reader, but not for the writer and/or typist. The biggest advantage to the reader is the convenience of having the source immediately available at the place where the material is used. The disadvantage for the writer and/or typist is spacing the page because the margins must be even at the bottom of the pages while meeting requirements of spacing for the footnotes themselves. An illustration of placing footnotes at the bottom of the page is the first page of a paper entitled "The Double Standard in Literary Criticism of the Nineteenth Century." (Note: The letters "rpt" in footnote 2 mean "reprinted by." See model footnote form on page 93.)

THE DOUBLE STANDARD IN LITERARY CRITICISM
OF THE NINETEENTH CENTURY

A double standard in literary criticism in the nineteenth century was one of the many difficulties both women
and novels faced while they were striving for serious
consideration. One scholar commented that

> all but the most enlightened of reviewers used
> one scale of merits for women writers and another
> for men. A woman was supposed to stay strictly
> within the limits of female delicacy in subject
> and style; in return she could expect from her
> reviewer the gallant treatment that a gentleman
> owes a lady: he would no more tell her that he
> disliked her novel than he would say that he could
> not stand the cut of her gown or the colour of
> her bonnet. Conversely, of course, she might be
> scolded for doing something, which, had she been
> a man, would have been praised.[1]

Accordingly, "novelists fell into three classes--men,
fair authoresses, and Grub-street hacks. . . ."[2] Fair
authoresses could write without social disgrace for only a
limited number of reasons: "moral zeal was an accepted
justification and poverty an accepted excuse. . . ."[3] As

---

[1]Inga-Stina Ewbank, Their Proper Sphere: A Study of
the Bronte Sisters as Early-Victorian Female Novelists
(Cambridge: Harvard University Press, 1966), p.2.

[2]J. M. S. Tompkins, The Popular Novel in England 1770-
1800 (1932, rpt Lincoln: University of Nebraska Press, 1961),
p. 127.

[3]Tompkins, p. 116.

Spacing for typing footnotes is as follows:

1. Double space after the last line of the text. Use the underline key for 15 spaces for the short, separating line.

2. Double space after the line.

3. Indent five spaces as for a paragraph.

4. Turn the typewriter platen back one-half space, hold, type the number, return to position. Do not space between the number and the first letter of the footnote. Follow the appropriate footnote form from among the models.

5. Single space as many lines as necessary for the footnote content.

6. Double space and repeat the procedure for the next footnote if there are more than one at the bottom of the page.

Listing footnotes on a separate page following the text of the paper is increasing in popularity because of its obvious convenience to the writer or typist. Many instructors are willing to put the footnote page beside the paper as they read and evaluate. You will find an example of the separate footnote page in Appendix A, the model research paper entitled "The Influences on the Music of Francis Vincent Zappa, Jr." The spacing for the footnotes themselves is the same as in their placement at the bottom of a page.

"Scientific notation" is used primarily in publications in the physical and behavioral sciences. Although most instructors in the humanities, history, English, and general studies courses in composition, literature, and various social studies do not accept this type of footnoting, one occasionally will, as the example shows.

In this system, the reference to the source is made in the text in parentheses. The parentheses will contain two items—either a number, as in the following illustration, or an author's last name, and a page number. If numbers are used, then the list of sources on the final bibliography page must be numbered as the key so the reader can find the author and title of the source. If the author's last name is used, it can be found on the bibliography page with the rest of the information about the publication.

The following example, using scientific notation, is taken from a paper entitled "The Beginning Writer':

```
When writing a novel, a beginning author is frequently

advised to write about material very familiar to him

and to set a regular schedule of two to four hours of

writing a day. "Any substantial increase in writing

ability arrives as a result of general growth plus

writing practice." (8:225) The beginning author is in
```

A variation of the form of scientific notation is to use the author's name and the year of the publication within the parentheses. Readers then locate the author and publication date on the bibliography page. Confusion can result when an author had more than one publication in a year.

```
The results of experiments on rhesus monkeys

showed them to be highly resistant to the virus.  (Rogers,

1968.)  Three other families of monkeys subjected to the
```

3. Footnote forms

Although the current academic trend is to simplify scholarly mechanics such as footnote forms, nevertheless the arrangement of the individual pieces of information in each form is inherited tradition. The best way to handle these mechanical details is to identify the type of source, find the model form for that type, then arrange each piece of information and the necessary punctuation to conform to that model. When your paper is typed, you must underline every title or name that appears here in *italics*.

Note the following idiosyncrasies:

1. When the place of publication (the home office of the publishing company) is a large, well-known city, do not include the state name. Boston, London, New York, and Chicago are a few examples. Put in the state if the town is small and unknown: Garden City, New York, or Glendale, Illinois, for example.

2. If the title page of the publication shows several cities under the publisher's name and no printing device, such as all capital letters, tells you which is home base, use the first one listed. If the city names are not alphabetized, the first one is usually the home office. If the city names are alphabetized, it's difficult to identify home base.

3. If the publisher is a university press and the place of publication is the town in which the main campus is located, don't include the state. For example, Lincoln: University of Nebraska Press, or Cambridge: Harvard University Press. It would be difficult to assume that Lincoln is in a state other than Nebraska or to confuse Cambridge, Massachusetts, with Cambridge, England, when Harvard is the next word. Use the same reasoning for Washington: Government Printing Office. "D.C." is not necessary.

The following models, based on the MLA Style Sheet, second edition, cover forms for the sources most frequently used in the majority of research papers.

- *Book or pamphlet with one author*

[1] Michael Pearson, *Those Damned Rebels: The American Revolution as Seen Through British Eyes* (New York: G. P. Putnam's Sons, 1972), p. 79.

- *Book or pamphlet with more than one author*

[2] Edward Rogers, William Wilson and Eugene Caston, *Mathematics Defined* (Chicago: University of Chicago Press, 1960), pp. 11–12.
  Or:
[2] Edward Rogers and others, *Mathematics Defined* (Chicago: University of Chicago Press, 1960), pp. 11–12.

- *Book or pamphlet with an editor*

[3] Jeffrey Hart, ed., *Political Writers of Eighteenth-Century England* (New York: Alfred Knopf & Co., 1964), pp. 176–178.

- *Reprint of an old book in hardback or paperback*

[4] J. M. S. Tompkins, *The Popular Novel in England 1770–1800* (1932, rpt Lincoln: University of Nebraska Press, 1961), p. 127.
(Note: 1932 was the original copyright date; "rpt" means "reprinted by"; the rest of the information is the current publishing data.)

- *Book or pamphlet with group, committee, or corporate author*

[5] U.S. Department of the Interior, *Threatened Wildlife of the United States* (Washington: Government Printing Office, 1973), p. 5.

- **Books in series**

[6] Donald G. Fink, *Computers and the Human Mind*, Science Study Series No. 43 (New York: Doubleday & Co., 1966), p. 135.

[7] Louis Bredvold, *The Literature of the Restoration and the Eighteenth Century: 1660–1798*, Vol. III in *A History of English Literature* (Oxford: University of Oxford Press, 1950), pp. 51–55.

- **Film or filmstrip**

[8] *Birds of the Prairie* (Blackhawk Film Co., 1972), film.

- **Recording**

[9] *The Ideal Teacher: A Scholarly Discussion* (Educational Research Group, 1970), tape.

- **Television documentary or special**

[10] Charles Collingwood, narrator, *Picasso Is 90* (New York: CBS News, 1971), documentary.
(Note: Home offices for all three television networks are in New York.)

- **Article from a monthly magazine or journal with individual page numbers for each issue**

[11] William T. Keeton, "The Mystery of Pigeon Homing," *Scientific American*, December 1974, pp. 99–100.

- **Article from a weekly magazine with no author given**

[12] "The Palestinian Tug of War," *Newsweek*, 4 November 1974, p. 37.

- *Article from a weekly magazine with author given*

[13] Richard Reeves, "The Senate Syndrome," *Newsweek*, 4 November 1974, p. 11.

- *Article from a journal with continuous page numbering through all issues of the volume*

[14] Peggy Rosenthal, "Feminism and Life in Feminist Biography," *College English*, 36 (1974), 182.

- *Article from a book of essays, readings, or an anthology*

[15] Dorothy Van Ghent, "On *Moll Flanders*," in *Essays on the Eighteenth Century Novel*, ed. Robert D. Spector (Bloomington: Indiana University Press, 1965), p. 5.

- *One cut from a record*

[16] Jimi Hendrix, "Third Stone From the Sun," *The Jimi Hendrix Experience* (Burbank, Cal.: Reprise Records, 1971), Side 1, Cut 3.

- *One record from an album*

[17] Helge Kokeritz, "Middle English," *A Thousand Years of English Pronunciation* (Pleasantville, N.Y.: Educational Audio Visual, 1961), Record 1, Side 2.

- *A quotation found in your source*

[18] As quoted in Frank Shay, *American Heroes of Legend and Lore* (1930, rpt New York: Pyramid Publications, 1964), p. 10.

[19] As quoted in Rose Styron, "Political Prisoners: When Death Seems a Lesser Evil," *Ms.*, January 1975, p. 60.

- *Newspaper article with no author*

[20] "Inflation Hurts India's Middle Class," *The New York Times*, 15 December 1974, Sec. 1, p. 2.

- *Newspaper article with author*

[21] M. A. Farber, "Ford Foundation to Slash Grants Over Next Four Years," *The New York Times*, 15 December 1974, Sec. 1, p. 30.

- *Newspaper editorial*

[22] "Congress Takes New Look at Foreign Aid," editorial in *The Cumberland* (Maryland) *News*, 17 December 1974, p. 9.

- *Newscast*

[23] John Chancellor, anchor, *NBC Nightly News*, 8 January 1975, 6:30 p.m.
[24] Heather Bernard, reporter, "Bomb Explosion at LaGuardia Airport," *NBC News*, 5 p.m., 30 December 1975.

Second, third, fourth, and all subsequent uses of the same source is a place where the current trend to simplification of scholarly mechanics is clearly evident. The use of Latin designations, such as *Ibid.*, *op. cit.*, and *loc. cit.*, for additional uses of the same source generally has been dropped from footnote forms. Therefore, to show second, third, fourth quotations or summarized material from the same source, use the author's last name and a page number. If no author is given in any kind of publication, use the title and page number. If the author is a committee, a department such as United States Department of Agriculture, or a corporate entity, use the title of the publication. Cut a long title to a few pertinent words. If you have two sources by the same author, use author's last name, title, and page number. The following are the models:

[3] Pearson, p. 90.

[6] "The Palestinian Tug of War," p. 38.

[9] Fishwick, *The Hero, American Style*, p. 177.

[10] Fishwick, "The Difficulty of Being a Hero," p. 39.

(Note: One source by Fishwick is a book; the other, a magazine article.)

[35] Bernard, 30 December 1975.

G. Bibliography Page Forms

The bibliography page completes the paper. Placed at the end, it contains one of the following two types of lists of sources:

1. A list of sources used in the paper.

2. A list of sources used in the paper as well as those read for information, but not quoted.

Which content your list contains depends upon the preferences of your instructor. However, the forms for both types of lists are the same.

The material on the bibliography page will be the third and final use of the publishing information of sources that started on a card in your working bibliography. The main differences between the footnote and bibliography page forms are punctuation and placement on the page. Compare the footnote form and the bibliography page form that follows for the most commonly used source—the book by a single author. You can see that the footnote form is treated as a sentence, with the items of information separated by commas. The bibliography page form is treated as an item in a catalogue list, with each element separated by periods. The placement on the page of the two forms is reversed. The footnote form is indented like a sentence at the beginning of a paragraph. The bibliography form, as a catalogue item, has the second, third, and subsequent lines indented.

- **Footnote form**

  [3] Sydney W. Head, *Broadcasting in America* (Boston: Houghton Mifflin, 1972), p. 63.

- **Bibliography page form**

Head, Sydney W. *Broadcasting in America.* Boston: Hough-ton Mifflin, 1972.

The bibliography page is titled and consists of an alphabetized list of sources. Alphabetize the items according to the last name of the author or, in case of no author, the first important word of the title.

Do not put page numbers in the bibliography forms for books. Put in both beginning and end page numbers for magazine articles. Make sure there is a period at the end of every item.

The following models parallel the model footnote forms:

- **Book or pamphlet with one author**

Pearson, Michael. *Those Damned Rebels: The American Revolution as Seen Through British Eyes.* New York: G. P. Putnam's Sons, 1972.

- *Book or pamphlet with more than one author*

Rogers, Edward, William Wilson and Eugene Caston. *Mathematics Defined*. Chicago: University of Chicago Press, 1960.
Or:
Rogers, Edward, and others. *Mathematics Defined*. Chicago: University of Chicago Press, 1960.

- *Book or pamphlet with an editor*

Hart, Jeffrey, ed. *Political Writers of Eighteenth-Century England*. New York: Alfred Knopf & Co., 1964.

- *Reprint of an old book in hardback or paperback*

Tompkins, J. M. S. *The Popular Novel in England 1770–1800*. 1932, rpt Lincoln: University of Nebraska Press, 1961.

- *Book or pamphlet with group, committee, or corporate author*

U.S. Department of the Interior. *Threatened Wildlife of the United States*. Washington: Government Printing Office, 1973.

- *Books in series*

Fink, Donald G. *Computers and the Human Mind*. Science Study Series No. 43. New York: Doubleday & Co., 1966.
Bredvold, Louis. *The Literature of the Restoration and the Eighteenth Century: 1660–1798*. Vol. III in *A History of English Literature*. Oxford: University of Oxford Press, 1950.

- *Television documentary or special*

Collingwood, Charles, narrator. *Picasso Is 90*. New York: CBS News, 1971.

- *Article from a monthly magazine or journal with individual page numbers for each issue*

Keeton, William T. "The Mystery of Pigeon Homing." *Scientific American*, December 1974, pp. 96–106.

- *Article from a weekly magazine with no author given*

"The Palestinian Tug of War." *Newsweek*, 4 November 1974, pp. 36–38.

- *Article from a weekly magazine with author given*

Reeves, Richard. "The Senate Syndrome." *Newsweek*, 4 November 1974, p. 11.

- *Article from a journal with continuous page numbering through all issues of the volume*

Rosenthal, Peggy. "Feminism and Life in Feminist Biography." *College English*, 36 (1974), 180–184.

- *Article from a book of essays, readings, or an anthology*

Van Ghent, Dorothy. "On *Moll Flanders*." In *Essays on the Eighteenth Century Novel*. Ed. Robert D. Spector. Bloomington: Indiana University Press, 1965.

- *One cut from a record*

Hendrix, Jimi. "Third Stone From the Sun." *The Jimi Hendrix Experience.* Burbank, Cal.: Reprise Records, 1971.

- *One record from an album*

Kokeritz, Helge. "Middle English." *A Thousand Years of English Pronunciation.* Pleasantville, N.Y.: Educational Audio Visual, Inc., 1961.

- *Newspaper article with no author*

"Inflation Hurts India's Middle Class." *The New York Times,* 15 December 1974, Sec. 1, p. 2.

- *Newspaper article with author*

Farber, M. A. "Ford Foundation to Slash Grants Over Next Four Years." *The New York Times,* 15 December 1974, Sec. 1, p. 30.

- *Newspaper editorial*

"Congress Takes New Look at Foreign Aid." Editorial in *The Cumberland* (Maryland) *News,* 17 December 1974, p. 9.

- *Newscast*

Chancellor, John, anchor. *NBC Nightly News,* 8 January 1975, 6:30 p.m.
Bernard, Heather, reporter. "Bomb Explosion at LaGuardia Airport." *NBC News,* 30 December 1975.

H. Illustrations, Maps, Charts, Diagrams

Illustrative materials can be placed either in the text of the paper where they are discussed or at the end. In either place, they should be numbered consecutively.

If the illustrations are too long or too complex to insert into the text, place them at the end of the paper, before the footnote page and/or bibliography page, named and lettered as follows: Appendix A, Appendix B, Appendix C. References to this material should be placed in the body of the paper in parentheses, as in (See Appendix A.), not in the footnotes.

Step 10: Format of Final Paper

1. Elements

The final paper should contain the following elements in this order:

1. Title page.

2. Body of the paper.

3. Illustrations.

4. Footnote page, if used.

5. Bibliography page.

It isn't necessary to put extra blank sheets between these elements. Whether or not you put the completed paper into a folder or plastic sheets will depend upon your instructor's preferences. Many like the folder, but others feel it slows down the reading and makes handling the paper clumsy, particularly if you have used the separate page for your footnotes.

2. Title page

Use the title page as illustrated in the two model research papers in Appendixes A and B. No additional information is necessary unless your instructor requests it.

3. Margins

Unless otherwise instructed, use an inch margin on all four sides of your paper. If you are typing on a pica typewriter, set the margins at 10 and 75. It is helpful to draw a frame in heavy black ink on a sheet of paper and use that as a guide under the page upon which you are typing. It keeps the top and bottom margins the same width throughout the paper.

4. Numbering pages

Do not number the first page. Start numbering the pages with page 2 by placing the numbers in the upper right corner several lines below the top of the sheet of paper and even with the right margin (i.e., one inch from the edge of the paper). Then number pages consecutively through the last page of the bibliography.

Step 11: Style of Writing

The following few items about writing style are worth noting:

1. Because this is a reasonably formal paper, if you have a doubt about the use of a word or phrase, stick to conservative grammatical usage. For example, don't use contractions like this one and the others in preceding pages. This manual is in a casual style; therefore, I have allowed myself greater freedom to use informal structures and expressions from conversation than I would in a research paper of my own. The same goes for punctuation. When in doubt, keep to the conservative usage.

2. Avoid frequent use of slang. A slang expression or two in a paper would not raise eyebrows nor lower grades, but ten slang expressions in the same paper would. It is wise to announce even your one or two expressions to your reader. You can say, "as the slang expression puts it, . . . ," or "to use the vernacular, . . . ," or "as expressed informally, . . ." Your reader then knows that you are aware of what you are doing.

3. The same warning applies to fragments—avoid using them. Even when you are deliberately and knowledgeably inserting a fragment for dramatic emphasis or clarity, your reader may not realize it. He or she might think you don't know the difference between a fragment and a complete sentence.

4. Do not hang sentences together on strings of commas like shirts pinned on a clothes line. These are comma splices, and the usage comes from casual conversation. Writing is different. If the ideas need to be held close together to show connection or rapid flow of events, use semicolons.

5. Do not use *so* as an intensifier. This is acceptable in casual conversation because tone of voice implies the rest of

the meaning. In writing, it is an incomplete sentence of degree. For example: Don't write "He was so good at his job." You must complete the sentence: "He was so good at his job that the company's president noticed him." In casual conversation, you can say, "He is soooo nice!" and everyone will understand the rest. It is true that you will find this usage in popular novels and magazines where the writing is colloquial and informal, but that is not the kind of writing you are doing in your research paper. Complete the sentence.

6. Avoid dangling comparatives. These are used so consistently in advertising that you have absorbed the usage through your pores and never question it. Lines such as "It gives more taste!" and "It has better flavor!" are constantly pouring out of television sets. In formal writing for research papers, the comparison must be completed. "It gives more taste than boiled cabbage." "It has better flavor than your next-door neighbor's weeds." These examples may be somewhat extreme, but that is the grammatical idea.

7. The use of "I" in the finished paper can be something of a problem, particularly if you are used to writing mostly personal experience essays. Although you have made the material your own and are not just copying sections of other people's writing, you must write impersonally. Do not use such expressions as "I think," "I am convinced," "It is my opinion that. . . ," or personal pronouns such as "my," "me," and "mine." Avoid also the editorial "we," the nineteenth-century "one," and such awkward disguises as "someone who has just started this kind of study," "this reporter," and "as a beginning student." And, for heaven's sake, don't ever write "I feel" in a research paper. Feelings

have no place in writing about objective material into which you have put deep, concentrated thought. Keep the writing impersonal by making simple declarations. For example, don't say, "In my opinion George Washington made an error of judgment." Say, "George Washington made an error of judgment." If the preceding paragraphs have been properly written, the fact that this is your opinion will be evident.

8. Don't use "etc." at the end of a series in a research paper. If you cannot think of any other examples, reasons, illustrations, or effects, just end the sentence. Putting "etc." at the end of a series is like dumping on someone else a job you didn't finish.

Step 12: Checking the Final Paper

While preparing the final version of your paper, look closely at your words and sentence structure. Read the paper aloud to someone. Careless errors will jump out and can be corrected. Evaluate closely in order to change, eliminate, and condense. Rewriting is not merely copying over. Find less wordy, more vivid ways to write. Your thought won't die if you slim it down and dress it up a bit. In fact, it may become as vivacious as a girl who just lost twenty pounds and bought a new dress to celebrate.

Allow some time between completing the final version and turning it in. During that time, proofread the paper as though you had never seen it before. It's very irritating and time-consuming to read a paper that has not been properly proofed. An instructor is frequently tempted, because of reading difficulty, just to count those typographical errors as misspellings.

The way to check footnote and bibliography page forms is to hold your paper against the forms in this manual and compare them element by element, punctuation mark by punctuation mark, to make sure you have duplicated the model exactly.

Afterword

There you have it. An even dozen steps to investigate, organize, and write a research paper. Unlike the advertising that claims just three simple steps, easy to do, and it's fun, too, writing a research paper is not easy; it is not simple; and I can't guarantee that it's even fun. I know that it can be interesting and tremendously rewarding in ways you don't imagine as you are doing it. I can promise you a feeling of pride, achievement, and self-confidence as you turn in the completed paper on time and without black bags under your eyes.

Appendix A

The following is a model research paper showing use of summary and direct quotations, with footnotes placed on a separate page. In addition, this paper shows how to incorporate audio and makes a cassette tape, which was submitted with the paper, an integral part of it.

When he prepared this paper, the student recorded short portions from various albums. These short excerpts are audio equivalents of written quotations. The student noted the sources in the traditional way on the footnote and bibliography pages and cued the reader when to listen to a section of the tape by inserting appropriate instructions in the text.

THE INFLUENCES ON THE MUSIC OF FRANCIS VINCENT ZAPPA, JR.

by

Joseph T. Cashwell

English 102, Section 6
City University College
April 2, 1976

111

THE INFLUENCES ON THE MUSIC OF FRANCIS VINCENT ZAPPA, JR.

Throughout the history of musicology, all composers
have either been influenced by their predecessors and adopted
an existing school of compositional style or, after being
influenced, have branched off, thus starting their own schools
of musical thought. Frank Zappa is one of the latter. He
is a contemporary pop-rhythm-blues-progressive jazz musician
whose musical style at first hearing appears to be a horrid
mixture of discordant noise and disgusting, vulgar lyrics.
However, Zappa's style, once analyzed, reveals definite
influences from the ideas and philosophies of three twentieth
century composers. Combined with his pubescent indoctrination
in rhythm and blues and the adolescent idiosyncrasies of the
1950s, the influences of these composers shaped an atypical
form of progressive jazz and jazz-rock that has marked Zappa
as one of the most individual and prolific jazz-rock composers
of the 1960s.

The three twentieth century composers who influenced
Zappa's music were Edgard Varèse (1883-1965), Igor Stravinsky
(1882-1965), and Anton Webern (1883-1945). Varèse, a Paris-
born American, experimented with sounds and noises that could
be incorporated into a composition as music. He thought of
music as ". . . bodies of intelligent sounds moving freely

112

in space. . . ."[1] His compositions involved various combinations of traditional instruments, as well as the invention
and use of new electronic and percussive instruments. Igor
Stravinsky, a Russian-born composer, was a writer of orchestral
music who used varieties of time signature and key changes
to achieve unusual effects. Stravinsky saw music ". . .as
a purely objective arrangement of pitches in time."[2] Anton
Webern, from Vienna, was a pupil of Arnold Schoenberg (1874-
1951). He took Schoenberg's system of twelve-tone music and
expanded it a step further. His music ". . . became the
inspiration for young progressive-minded composers all over
the world--not only composers of serious music, but even
composers of [progressive] jazz."[3] These three different
styles were combined with Zappa's basic style of rock.

Zappa's basic style of rock music was influenced by
". . . electric rhythm and blues between 1953 and 1958. . . ."[4]
A large proportion of his adolescent earnings was invested
in the records of musicians such as Johnny Otis and Willie
May Thornton. He listened to these recordings over and
over again, getting from them his earliest musical influence
and direction. From these evolved his basic format. His
music was to follow the lead these musicians started and
fall into the general classification of rock, but the
added influences of Varèse, Stravinsky and Webern created
a rock style that was ahead of its time in 1965.

Of the variety of influences on Zappa's music, the impact
of Edgard Varèse on all but the basic rock format is perhaps
the most easily heard and recognized. Zappa has identified

113

Varèse's influence in articles he has written about the composer and by using a statement made by Varèse in 1921, "The present-day composer refuses to die," on the majority of his album covers. Varèse once said of his music, "I dream of instruments obedient to my thought and which, with their contributions of a whole new world of unsuspected sounds, will lend themselves to the exigencies of my inner rhythm."[5] Zappa has said, "I liked [Varèse's] music because it sounded good to me."[6] The sound of Varèse's music is the first selection on the accompanying tape. (Play tape, section 1.)[7]

Zappa incorporated Varèse's musical experiments in the form of preludes to more structured rock compositions. On his album, We're Only In It For The Money, the piece on side two, "Nasal Retentive Calliopie Music," incorporates electronic sounds as well as studio-created effects (i.e., the sounds of surf on the beach and of a phonograph needle being gouged into a record) into a structured piece of music. Combined with the effects of stereo separation, the work invokes not only a high degree of bizarre musical humor, but also an ordered, quasi-cadential introduction to the next piece on the album, "Let's Make The Water Turn Black," a more tonal piece of music. (Play tape, section two.)[8] On his album, Weasels Ripped My Flesh, Zappa uses electronic sounds as an independent composition entitled, "Dwarf Nebula Processional March and Dwarf Nebula." After a brief instrumental introduction, the song moves into a section of electronic effects involving speeded-up sections of prerecorded tapes and the guttural tone qualities of the human voice.

(Play tape, section three.)[9] Zappa's music, though not totally matching the achievements of Varèse's, shows that he took Varèse's philosophy and ideas and introduced them to the rock world.

Igor Stravinsky and the realm of traditional instrumentation entered Zappa's life early and appear in his music. Stravinsky used orchestra tone color, tonal dissonance and varieties of time and key signature changes in his work. (Play tape, section four.)[10] Zappa, using a symphony orchestra to augment his regular troupe of musicians, some of whom had degrees in traditional instruments themselves, composed extremely colorful and innovative pieces for the rock world. In his album, Lumpy Gravy, "a curiously inconsistent piece which started out to be a ballet but probably didn't make it,"[11] Zappa, conducting the Abnucleas Ekuukha Electric Symphony Orchestra, used Stravinsky's devices to produce a highly orchestrated and very colorful style of rock music. (Play tape, section five.)[12] In the soundtrack for his movie, 200 Motels, Zappa, using the Royal Philharmonic Orchestra, demonstrates his talents as a composer, and the work best exemplifies the influence of Stravinsky on his music. The overture and several of the dances are scored for orchestra alone and show Zappa's ability to create music without the need for a rock ensemble. (Play tape, section six.)[13]

Anton Webern, a Viennese composer, influenced Zappa by using and extending Arnold Schoenberg's twelve-tone system of music. (Play tape, section seven.)[14] This style of music, which, to the untrained listener, sounds like a group of musicians playing without coordination, caught Zappa's interest, and in his early twenties, he composed several atonal works. Adapting Webern's methods required rearranging the chromatic musical scale so that the individual musical tones play off each other's dissonant tone. Using this style, Zappa's jazz progressions became group improvisational efforts. However, when he heard some of these performed, he was disappointed. He said, "I didn't like it. I knew the serial integrity was there, but nobody else was going to hear the mathematics that went into it."[15] Nonetheless, Zappa continued to seriously compose atonal music and used some short pieces on his albums. (Play tape, section eight.)[16]

Like most underground music of the sixties, Zappa's was a commentary on the social problems of the time. With the musical techniques of Varèse, Stravinsky, Webern, and the rhythm and blues musicians encountered in his adolescence as the basis for his musical format, Zappa tied them to his observation of the lifestyles he saw developing in Los Angeles and San Francisco to create a poignant and sometimes brutal form of musical satire on contemporary topics such as, for example, the "hippie" movement. (Play tape, section nine.)[17] The following lyric describes how Zappa saw some of the counterfeit qualities of the teenage "hippie" movement.

> Walked past the wig store
> Danced at the Fillmore
> I'm completely stoned
> I'm hippy and I'm trippy
> I'm a gypsy on my own
> I'll stay a week and get the crabs and
> Take the bus back home
> I'm really just a phony
> But forgive me
> 'Cause I'm stoned . . .[18]

Stravinsky's, Varèse's and Webern's musical techniques, combined with Zappa's satire, fit smoothly together. The singers used vocal distortion and harmonic dissonance to flavor the music with a biting pungency that brought the theme of the lyrics across. Frank Zappa and his Mothers of Invention became the satirists of the adolescent cultural movement of the late sixties, particularly during the "Summer of Love," lambasting and lampooning parents, police, politicians and the general attitudes of America. (Play tape, section ten.) [19]

Although Varèse, Stravinsky and Webern are today considered outstanding masters in their areas of music, at the time they were composing, their music was harshly criticized because it went against accepted musical standards. Zappa, who considers himself to be "a composer who plays guitar," [20] fell victim of the same kind of criticism during the late sixties, but he and his music have persevered. "Zappa is a true environmental artist. He picks up on vibes. He takes whatever his environment happens to be and exploits it to its fullest degree." [21] Zappa has described his own work as follows:

> The greatest fun I can have is finding the most
> dissimilar elements and hooking them all together
> so it [the musical composition] will work. Any-
> thing that seems completely impossible. I mean,
> my whole life is devoted to doing things like that:
> taking the most absurd concepts and turning them
> into reality. [22]

Zappa took from his influences, musical and environ-mental, what he needed to create a musical format that made him an outstanding creative genius in the rock movement.

117

Musicians are today developing further the styles and forms
Zappa began, and they also might run into adverse criticism.
However, Zappa--the musician, the composer, the satirist--
has shown what can be accomplished by consolidating comple-
mentary styles of music, and he will be remembered as one
of the great masters of rock.

FOOTNOTES

[1]Elliot Schwartz and Barney Childs, eds., _Contemporary Composers on Contemporary Music_ (New York: Holt, Rinehart and Winston, 1967), p. 204.

[2]Schwartz and Childs, p. 48.

[3]David Ewen, _Composers of Tomorrow's Music_ (New York: Dodd, Mead and Company, 1971), p. 74.

[4]Craig McGregor, "Zapparap on the Zappaplan," _The New York Times_, 8 November 1970, Sec. 2, p. 29.

[5]Eric Salsman, "Edgard Varèse," _Stereo Review_, June 1971, p. 59.

[6]David Walley, _No Commercial Potential_ (New York: Outerbridge and Lazard, Inc., 1972), p. 27.

[7]Edgard Varèse, "Hyperism," and "Poème Electronique," _The Varèse Album_ (New York: Columbia Records, no date) Record I, Side 1, Cuts 2 and 3.

[8]The Mothers of Invention, _We're Only In It For The Money_ (Hollywood, Cal.: Verve Records, 1967), Side 2, Cut 1.

[9]The Mothers of Invention, "Dwarf Nebula Processional March and Dwarf Nebula," _Weasels Ripped My Flesh_ (Burbank, Cal.: Bizarre Records, 1970), Side 2, Cut 1.

[10]Igor Stravinsky, "The Rite of Spring," _Stravinsky: His Finest Music_ (U.S.A.: Sine Qua Non, no date), Record 2, Side 2.

[11]Frank Zappa, _Lumpy Gravy_ (Hollywood, Cal.: Verve Records, 1967), background notes.

[12]Zappa, _Lumpy Gravy_, Side 1.

[13]Frank Zappa, "Semi-Fraudulent/Direct-From/Hollywood Overture," _200 Motels_ (Los Angeles: United Artists, 1971), Side 1, Cut 1; "Dance of the Rock and Roll Interviewers," Side 1, Cut 3; "Dance of the Just Plain Folks," Side 1, Cut 6; and "Lucy's Seduction of a Bored Violinist and Postlude," Side 2, Cut 10.

[14]Anton Webern, "Concerto, Opus 20," _The Complete Works_ (New York: Columbia Records, no date), Side 6, Cut 1.

[15]Walley, p. 28.

[16]The Mothers of Invention, "Igor's Boogie, Phase One and Phase Two," Burnt Weenie Sandwich (Burbank, Cal.: Bizarre Records, 1969), Side 1, Cut 5.

[18]The Mothers of Invention, "Who Needs the Peace Corps," We're Only In It For The Money, Side 1, Cut 2.

[19]The Mothers of Invention, Absolutely Free (Hollywood, Cal.: Verve Records, 1967), Sides 1 and 2.

[20]Walley, p. 9.

[21]Walley, p. 3.

[22]McGregor, p. 29.

BIBLIOGRAPHY

Ewen, David. Composers of Tomorrow's Music. New York: Dodd, Mead and Company, 1971.

McGregor, Craig. "Zapparap on the Zappaplan." The New York Times, 8 November 1970, Section 2, pp. 17, 29, and 33.

Mothers of Invention, The. Absolutely Free. Hollywood, Cal., Verve Records, 1967.

_____. Burnt Weenie Sandwich. Burbank, Cal.: Bizarre Records, 1969.

_____. Cruisin' With Ruben and the Jets. Hollywood, Cal.: Verve Records, 1968.

_____. Weasels Ripped My Flesh. Burbank, Cal.: Bizarre Records, 1970.

_____. We're Only In It For The Money. Hollywood, Cal.: Verve Records, 1967.

Salsman, Eric. "Edgard Varèse." Stereo Review, June 1971, pp. 62-63.

Schwartz, Elliot, and Barney Childs, eds. Contemporary Composers on Contemporary Music. New York: Holt, Rinehart and Winston, 1967.

Stravinsky, Igor. "The Rite of Spring." Stravinsky: His Finest Music. U.S.A.: Sine Qua Non, no date.

Varèse, Edgard. The Varèse Album. New York: Columbia Records, no date.

Walley, David. No Commercial Potential. New York: Outerbridge and Lazard, 1972.

Webern, Anton. "Concerto, Opus 20." The Complete Works. New York: Columbia Records, no date.

Zappa, Frank. Lumpy Gravy. Hollywood, Cal.: Verve Records, 1967.

_____. 200 Motels. Los Angeles: United Artists, 1971.

Appendix B

The following is a literary paper showing the use of a novel as primary source.

CLARISSA AND LOVELACE: THE PROBLEMS
OF AN EIGHTEEN-YEAR-OLD GIRL

by

Linda Jean Henry

English 103, Section 12
City University College
January 15, 1976

CLARISSA AND LOVELACE: THE PROBLEMS OF AN EIGHTEEN-YEAR-OLD GIRL

Before Clarissa's evolving attitude toward Lovelace can be explained, Samuel Richardson's main emphasis in the novel must be identified. Is Clarissa, or The History of a Young Lady, a novel of love and marriage? Morality and immorality? Or social examination and warning?

To the twentieth-century mind, placing the adolescent elements of Clarissa's age, parental restraints, family demands for "cheerful" obedience and concern for money opposite a popular girl's joyously fearful delight in controlling a "bad" man, Lovelace's inexhaustible inventiveness and continuous glandular excitation in the name of love, and all the main characters' obsessive concern with marriage, the decision must be that this is a novel of love and marriage. Isn't that all they talk about?

Being content with that decision, however, would be like accepting the meringue for the pie. Yet, to say that the novel's main emphasis is morality and immorality would be equally superficial. In spite of the pages of moral precepts that Richardson presented to his readers after ten years of revisions and additions, he built originally on a deeper, firmer foundation than perhaps he himself knew. If he wrote

126

Pamela because of his concern for the unprotected servant girl's dangers in the eighteenth-century social structure, would he be unconcerned about the affluent girl's dangers in the same structure--particularly when the dangers were virtually the same and the affluent girl had more to lose? Pamela had only her virtue at stake, but Clarissa had virtue, a large fortune, her personal reputation, and her family's social position to lose. Each girl was forced to rely for "protection" on the man who was her worst enemy and, for Clarissa, her ultimate doom.

In the context of both novels, but more seriously in Clarissa, the word "protection" acts as the key to Richardson's main emphasis. Although he was concerned with morality, he seemed more deeply concerned with social examination and warning. His moral precepts, in this context, by prescribing behavior to ward off trouble, can be construed as warnings against the dangers of his time, dangers that stemmed from even a rich girl's vulnerability to lack of legal, social, and personal restraint of men in a male-dominated social structure. Clarissa lacked control over her person, fortune, and life. The few protective property laws discriminated against all but first sons; none protected women. The first protective civil marriage law was not enacted by Parliament until 1753. Before then, a marriage's legality was in the hands of individual priests and ministers. Pamela lives in fear of a "sham" marriage by a poseur in priest's clothing. From Lovelace's other actions, we can assume that he forged

127

the marriage license and that the minister he frequently
offers to call in will be another imposter. Clarissa had
to ask her father for permission to "live single," and,
although she says she turned her grandfather's estate over
to her father's "bounty," chances are that this was an empty
gesture. Her male trustees, if agreed among themselves,
could have done as they chose. The fact of Lovelace's
larger fortune is nullified by Clarissa's lack of legal
control over her own, particularly after she left her father's
"protection."

Coupling these facts of existence with a social atmos-
phere of amused tolerance and underlying admiration for the
affluent young man's rakish escapades that were accepted as
the proper prelude to marriage and responsibility, the
eighteenth-century affluent young girl was very much in need
of protection when an unbalanced scoundrel came along.

Of equal importance to permissive rakishness for males
in the eighteenth-century social structure were the restric-
tive morés governing affluent young girls' behavior. Though
she didn't take advantage of it, Pamela factually had more
freedom of choice and movement than Clarissa. Even with
Richardson's possible misunderstanding of "high class"
decorum and the codes holding in thrall a gentleman's behavior, he knew thoroughly the manner-barriers that held Clarissa
as much prisoner as did Lovelace.

Taking these eighteenth-century conditions of life as
the foundation upon which Richardson built, his main emphasis

was social examination and warning. In this context, then,
the conflicts, barriers, choices, and penalties that faced
Clarissa become clear, and her evolving attitude toward
Lovelace can be identified and traced.

Within the clearly marked boundaries of her family's
protection, Clarissa was fearless. As far as she knew life,
she controlled her own destiny. Because she was a favorite
granddaughter, daughter, and niece, used to special prerogatives, she doubted not that her desires dictated her father's
and uncles' final decisions. That was life as Clarissa
Harlowe knew it for eighteen years. If not a spoiled and
willful eighteen-year-old, she was secure, confident, poised,
sure of her position and prerogatives, not unlike Jane Austen's
Emma Woodhouse, but with a tragically different destiny in
store for her.

Under these circumstances, then, she could safely play
the dangerous rake at the end of a long line. She could tell
Miss Howe, and later her family, that she answered Lovelace's
letters "purely to prevent further mischief."[1] She could
debate Lovelace's good and bad points, the possibility of
his reformation, and confess "a conditional kind of liking,"
(p. 48) to her confidante. She could toy with the idea of
accepting Lovelace when Mr. Solmes became such a repulsive
alternative. As long as she was the protected favorite

---

[1]Samuel Richardson, Clarissa, or The History of a Young
Lady, abridged and edited by George Sherburn (Boston: Hough-
ton Mifflin, 1962), p. 44. All subsequent citations from
this novel refer to this edition.

child, she diplomatically but fearlessly expressed her opinions and made decisions that she thought were real and binding upon others.

Clarissa's confidence began to crumble as she realized her wishes were ineffectual in deciding the most important matter in her life--her marriage. As she told Miss Howe, "Only one thing must be allowed for me; that whatever course I shall be _permitted_ or _forced_ to steer, I must be considered as a person out of her own direction," (p. 89) and then describes herself as "tossed to and fro by the high winds of passionate control." (p. 89)

As her control at home is slipping away from her, Clarissa shows that she thinks she is still controlling Lovelace by her annoyance when he lets a day go by before picking up a letter (pp. 90-91) and, later, after she said she would go away with him, when he does not remain at the rock to see if she had any other ideas, instructions, considerations, or changes of mind. (p. 124)

After Lovelace has panicked Clarissa into running away and she deduces the trickery, her confidence is irrevocably shattered. She told Miss Howe, "And what vexes me more is, that it is plain to me now, by all his behaviour, that he had as great a confidence in my weakness as I had in my own strength . . . he has not been mistaken in me, while I have in myself!" (p. 135)

Although she puts up a good fight, thereafter Clarissa's course is all downhill. Little by little, she realizes that she has neither control over this man nor protection from him, and she begins to fear him. "But here is the thing: I behold him with _fear_ now, as conscious of the power my indiscretion has given him over me." (p. 145) As Clarissa's fear begins to grow, so does her hatred of Lovelace. After her abortive escape to Hampstead, when she finds herself once again outside Mrs. Sinclair's "vile" house and nothing she says or does controls the coachman or the women who are relentlessly sweeping her back into her prison on waves of phony promises, helpless, she knows the depths of true fear and deep hatred. In her unprotected condition, the victim of Lovelace's villainy, drugged and raped, her feelings toward him become unalterable terror and revulsion.

Later, free but dying, she looks back with vestiges of her old spirited imperiousness to what might have been, had she not left what could be called her protected freedom. She wrote Mrs. Norton, "_I will own to you, that once I could have loved him--ungrateful man!--had he permitted me to love him, I once could have loved him._" (p. 345) Belford reported to Lovelace, "Poor man, said she: I once could have loved him. This is saying more than ever I could say of any other man out of my own family," (p. 464) and we know the length of her journey from the protected pleasures of ambiguous possibilities to terror and hatred, a hatred all the more intense because it was fueled by helplessness --the helplessness of facing a reality over which she had no control and no man in whom she could identify something paternal and protective.

Throughout this novel, Richardson emphasizes over and
over the importance of familial protection of a young girl,
because only a strong family could wield strong legal and
social control. By Clarissa's fate, he warns girls to stay
within the circle of protection. By the Harlowes' fate, he
warns families to protect their daughters better and not to
force them into marriages against their will. By Lovelace's
fate, he warns young rakes to change their ways. Within the
novel, Clarissa's attitude toward Lovelace evolves from
attraction and possible love to terror and absolute hatred,
with a little contemptuous pity to make a blend. As she
wrote Miss Howe:

> Let me then repeat, that I truly despise
> this man! If I know my own heart, indeed I
> do! I pity him! Beneath my very pity as he
> is, I nevertheless pity him! But this I could
> not do, if I still loved him: for, my dear,
> one must be greatly sensible of the baseness
> and ingratitude of those we love. I love him
> not, therefore! My soul distains communion
> with him. (p. 393)

To identify the date of her real death, Clarissa had carved
into her coffin the day she left the protection of her
home.